Kate O'Brien

Twayne's English Authors Series

TEAS 471

KATE O'BRIEN by James Sleator (1889—1950), oil on linen.
Gift of Miss O'Brien (1965) to the Permanent Collection of the
Limerick City Gallery of Art

Kate O'Brien

by Adele M. Dalsimer

Twayne Publishers
A Division of G.K. Hall & Co. ● *Boston*

823
0132zd

Published in the United States by
Twayne Publishers
A division of G.K. Hall & Co.
70 Lincoln Street,
Boston, Massachusetts 02111
© Adele M. Dalsimer, 1990

The author and publishers express their thanks to the Estate of Kate O'Brien
and to her publishers for permission to use copyright material as follows:
My Ireland: Batsford/Heinemann/Doubleday/Virago; *Without My Cloak:*
Heinemann/Doubleday/Virago; *Presentation Parlour:* Heinemann; *The Ante-Room:*
Heinemann/Doubleday/Arlen House; *Mary Lavelle:* Heinemann/Doubleday/
Virago; *Farewell, Spain:* Heinemann/Virago; *Pray for the Wanderer:* Heinemann/
Doubleday/Penguin; *The Land of Spices:* Heinemann/Doubleday/Arlen House;
The Last of Summer: Heinemann/Doubleday/Arlen House; *That Lady:* Heinemann/
Virago/Doubleday (under the title *For One Sweet Grape); The Flower of May:*
Heinemann/Harper; *As Music and Splendour:* Heinemann/Harper.

Print origination Typeworkshop Ltd.
Printed by The Camelot Press, Southampton.

Index by Helen Litton

Library of Congress Cataloguing in Publication Data
Dalsimer, Adele.
    Kate O'Brien/ by Adele M. Dalsimer.
    p. cm. - (Twayne's English authors series: TEAS 471)
    Includes bibliographical references.
    ISBN 0-8057-6994-3
    1. O'Brien, Kate, 1897-1974—Criticism and
interpretation. 1.Title. II. Series.
PR6029.B65Z64   1989
823'.912   dc20

For my family

Contents

About the Author

Adele M. Dalsimer is an Associate Professor of English and Co-Director of the Irish Studies Program at Boston College. She earned her B.A. from Mount Holyoke College, M.A. from Hunter College, and Ph.D. from Yale University.

Professor Dalsimer published *The Unappeasable Shadow: Shelley's Influence on Yeats* (Garland Publishing) in 1988. Her essay 'Hell and Parnassus by the Canal Bank: Patrick Kavanagh's Dublin' appeared in *The Irish Writer and the City,* ed. Maurice Harmon (Colin Smythe, 1984). She discovered and published an edition of T.H. Nally's presumably lost play, *The Spancel of Death* (Irish Studies, 1983) which had been scheduled to be performed on Easter Monday, 1916, when the Irish Uprising forced the Abbey Theatre to close. Professor Dalsimer has published numerous articles on Irish poetry and drama.

Acknowledgments

I wish to thank Professor Robin Lydenberg of Boston College for her consistent encouragement and intellectual support throughout the various stages of this book. Her belief in the project, her careful reading of numerous drafts, and her insightful comments about Kate O'Brien's works were invaluable. M. Jeanne Smith and Frances Givelber made their psychological understanding available to me at every turn, and to them both I am deeply grateful. I hope that my colleague Professor Kevin O'Neill will recognise the essential influence that our many years of working together have had on this study. A Faculty Fellowship from Boston College in 1987 made the completion of the manuscript possible, and the able assistance of Margaret Kelleher and Naomi Rosenberg made its preparation painless. My husband Jim read the manuscript when it mattered most, and his pleasure in it sustained me to the end. For him, I am always thankful.

Chapter One appeared as 'A Not So Simple Saga: Kate O'Brien's *Without My Cloak*' in *Eire-Ireland* XXI:3 (Fall 1986): 55-72.

Preface

Kate O'Brien is a pioneer. She is the first writer of Irish fiction to represent fully and meticulously the Catholic upper-middle class. And her innovation goes further. She is the first to address issues common among Irish women of the twentieth century and to introduce into Irish literature questions of female autonomy, self-definition, and sexual freedom that current writers, such as Edna O'Brien, Julia O'Faolain, and Val Mulkerns continue to address. Further still, she tenders the earliest female version of the Irish artistic quest that serves as a compelling analogue to the masculine experience explored initially by James Joyce, in *A Portrait of the Artist as a Young Man,* and later by such writers as Sean O'Faolain, in *Bird Alone,* and John McGahern, in *The Dark.* And finally, as deeply committed to Ireland as any of her male literary colleagues, residents and expatriates alike, Kate O'Brien scrutinises, even from long distance, the dominant social and political problems that beset her homeland. As do many of her male contemporaries, she consistently portrays the land and *mentalité* she sought to escape. But Kate O'Brien's Ireland differs profoundly from theirs, and her singular perspective warrants a prominent place in Irish letters.

Yet for all this, Kate O'Brien has been virtually ignored. Until only very recently, her books have been out of print and her achievements disregarded. Bourgeois in the Irish peasant state, Irish in the English literary world, a Catholic who lived for many years in a Protestant country, a woman, and a writer whose final novel explicitly portrays a lesbian relationship, Kate O'Brien was relegated to literary oblivion. The neglect of her works was such that Peter Costello could recently assert, 'It is remarkable that though the peasants, workers, and gentry all produced writers [in the decades immediately following the establishment of the Free State] . . . . there seems to have been no one writing about the middle classes, the new masters of Ireland.'[1]

Though more prosperous than most of Ireland's 'new masters', Kate O'Brien's subjects belong to the group of which Costello speaks, and, were it not for this author, their territory might well have remained uncharted in fiction. Readers of eighteenth- and nineteenth-century Irish literature are familiar with a divided social landscape: on one side, the

Protestant Big House, inhabited by a dissolute squire or an absentee landlord's grasping agent; on the other, the cottages of impoverished Catholic tenant farmers, the cabins of starving labourers, and the village houses of the Catholic doctor, lawyer, or gombeen man, coveting the Big House. To this scene, Irish writing of the twentieth century adds the urban tenement whose working-class inhabitants, Catholic and Protestant alike, struggle for survival and self-respect in a new terrain of physical and cultural deprivation. Only Kate O'Brien's novels offer a different view of post-Famine Ireland and identify the affluent, powerful Catholic business and professional men and their families who belonged to the upper-middle class. Joyce, in *The Dead* and the opening pages of *A Portrait of the Artist as a Young Man,* gives us merely elegiac glimpses.

Kate O'Brien traces in fine, filigreed detail the inhabitants of the new Catholic Big House, who survived the Famine and prospered through the turn of the century. She documents their apathy before national events disrupt it. The Ireland of her early novels is, as Eavan Boland has described,

Catholic Ireland: never nationalist Ireland. An Ireland that lay between the bankruptcies of Maria Edgeworth and the settled acres of Mary Lavin. A country where the women used rouge and talked about the price of muslin and the men smoked their cigars and discussed horse-flesh. It is a constituency which rejected Parnell, which turned its back on Redmond, which abhorred the Land League and had more in common with the oppressors than the oppressed. A selfish, limited, insular class.[2]

Her later novels portray subsequent generations of this privileged group, which, although somewhat less affluent than their forebears, continue to flourish as landholders and professionals, pillars of the new State and of the Church. Kate O'Brien's works testify to the tenacity of the Irish *haute bourgeoisie* despite a social ethos that differed in many respects from that of the newly formed Free State. The men and women about whom she writes would have scoffed at the idea of a 'peasant republic'.

Like Joyce, Kate O'Brien lived in self-imposed exile, obsessed not only with her homeland but particularly with her family's milieu. She sets six of her nine novels amid the Irish Catholic bourgeoisie, and in all but one, the central characters are Irish. In the novels that take place abroad, she focuses on the clash between her heroines' Irish middle-class values and their new social stimuli. Ireland, and especially Limerick, where she spent her early years, provides the standard by which Kate O'Brien gauges all other experience. In a personal and highly idiosyncratic travel book, *My Ireland,* published late in her life, she describes a bond to Limerick that strongly resembles Joyce's ties to Dublin:

'The freest spirit must have some birthplace, some *locus standi* from which to view the world and some innate passion by which to judge it.'

Modestly I say the same for my relationship with Limerick. It was there that I began to view the world and to develop the necessary passion by which to judge it. It was there indeed that I learnt the world, and I know that wherever I am it is still from Limerick that I look out and make my surmises. And, 'to possess without being possessed' — that may seem unfair, but it is the gift an exile can take from a known place, and more enriching, or so the recipient thinks, than the average portion of the stay-at-home.[3]

But the social perspective Kate O'Brien took from Limerick differed from the one Joyce brought from Dublin. He abandoned the bourgeois milieu of his early years and set his novels in lower middle-class Dublin to which his family's fortunes had led him. Kate O'Brien, on the other hand, lost none of her fascination with the world into which she was born and could have lived. The Irish Catholic bourgeoisie remained the touchstone of her imaginative vision.

Kate O'Brien's portrait is ambivalent, however. Like middle-class characters depicted in English novels, Kate O'Brien's dwell in ease and comfort in large homes in the suburbs of Mellick, the fictional equivalent of her native Limerick. Tribal loyalty and a strict adherence to Catholic doctrine are as expected in Mellick as beautiful clothes and rich furnishings. The family is at the centre of communal life; Catholicism is the anchor of unquestioned orthodoxy and cohesive moral standard. Indifferent to issues beyond their doors, Kate O'Brien's characters enjoy lives ruled more by bloodlines and belief than by public affairs and politics. They ignore, even scorn, the less privileged, and neither poverty nor violence, so devastating a part of Irish daily life — and fiction — intrudes. Outsiders cannot enter; insiders cannot leave.

In Mellick, as it must have felt to Kate O'Brien in Limerick, every positive has a negative. She shows how family members possess each other as jealously as they possess their material wealth, how women belong to men, children to their parents, and everyone to the Church. Family love is protective, but it is also smothering; religion consoles, but it also represses. Mellick prohibits and denies every nonconforming thought or deed. In the end, Kate O'Brien depicts a society in which self-fulfilment and self-expression are, especially for noncompliant women, impossible outside the family and often improbable within it.

Both as woman and as artist, Kate O'Brien finds untenable the limitations of the world her novels bring to life. She constructs her plots around the eruption of defiance or deviance and the conflicts it produces within a haven of domesticity and piety. Her heroines — in all but two of her novels her central characters are female — aware of the cost, fight against family, faith, and society. They remain deeply attached even as they struggle to separate. They can never reclaim what they leave in Mellick — and Kate O'Brien insists that leaving Mellick is inevitable and necessary if her heroines are to define themselves. We see their struggles — intense, painful, and in many ways, insurmountable — as Kate O'Brien's struggles as well. Her ambivalence toward Ireland is apparent even in her last years when, living in England, she contributed an occasional column to the *Irish Times*. Its title, 'Long Distance', captures both her need to remain apart and her wish to stay in touch.

Given her obsession with the relationship between one's girlhood and one's womanhood, we should not be surprised that Kate O'Brien devoted her entire career to the quest for freedom and its consequences. Each of her novels contributes to the search. Collectively, they lead the reader from the middle of the nineteenth century into the second quarter of the twentieth; from the province into which Kate O'Brien was born into the larger world where she sought acceptance. This movement outward, from past to present to future, from Ireland to Spain and Europe, is typical of Kate O'Brien's expanding perspective. For as her novels chronicle the search for personal and artistic freedom, they invariably set the individual within a larger social and political context. Kate O'Brien rejects self-absorption for social involvement, solipsism for historical awareness.

Her first public work, the play *Distinguished Villa,* staged in 1926, five years before her first novel was published, proclaims the central theme to which all her novels speak. Set in Brixton, a London suburb, the play is a stinging indictment of the social control of the bourgeoisie, far more condemnatory and caustic than any of her novels (except, perhaps, *The Last of Summer*). Thoroughly and fiercely negative, *Distinguished Villa* dramatises the morbidity of middle-class convention and the deathblow it deals to creativity. In her play, Kate O'Brien demonstrates that doing 'the right thing' may not be 'the best thing',[4] if superficial and tendentious morality determines the 'right thing'. The heroine, Frances Llewellyn, a librarian and writer who enjoys 'looking on' (26), is Kate O'Brien's prototypical female character, and possibly, a self-portrait. Independent, unconventional, reflective, Frances establishes the dilemma faced by all the women in Kate O'Brien's novels when she abandons love to preserve appearances and moves on. Brave and alone, Frances begins the wandering peculiar to Kate O'Brien's later heroines. Several will make similar sacrifices to ensure their individuality; others will fight to retain love and, in their defiance, maintain their unconventionality.

The stringent social codes of the Irish *haute bourgeoisie* are subtle but as binding as those that restrict the English lower-middle class, the milieu of Kate O'Brien, the playwright. Although the demands and effects of religious faith, family loyalties, and societal expectations change somewhat throughout her era, Kate O'Brien portrays the ways in which they still severely suppress talented, self-reliant women. Her novels quietly protest against the fates of middle-class Irish women who are sheltered, stifled, and forced into prescribed roles as wives, mothers, or spinsters who must care for ageing parents. Her most extreme portrayals depict the lives of women starved by a lack of passion or driven to their deaths by its excess. As mothers, Kate O'Brien's characters, denied educations, careers, even political opinions, frequently lose themselves in the lives of their children. Her more contemporary heroines, too, are constricted by the Free State's rigidly Catholic, confessional ethos and their own middle-class ideology.

Towards the end of her career, Kate O'Brien goes so far as to write about women who loosen the reins of Irish bourgeois morality not only in their search for individual and professional liberation or in their choice of sexual freedom and partner, but in the expression of a forbidden lesbian identity. In her early novels, *Without My Cloak* and *Mary Lavelle,* secondary characters appear on the periphery of conventional society, exiled by their homosexuality. In *The Land of Spices,* the central character is driven into a convent by the discovery of her father's affair with his male student. In her final two novels, *The Flower of May* and *As Music and Splendour,* Kate O'Brien's heroines reject heterosexual love in favour of female attachment and estrange themselves from Ireland.

Although as a female Irish novelist, Kate O'Brien is remarkably ahead of her time in treating such issues with candour and equanimity, she relies on inherently regressive ideas to formulate her arguments. She insists that her heroines must be free if they are to find and be themselves. At the same time, however, she insists that, despite the restraints familial bonds impose, they are always more real, more reliable, more lasting than the passionate attraction of mature adults. Kate O'Brien refuses to accept the idealisation of romantic love; the nostalgic pull to family and past proves irresistible.

Sometimes wistfully, sometimes bitterly, her novels wrap Mellick in a tribalism that makes its citizens appear as an extended family, and marriages among families, such as the Considines and the Hennessys in *Without My Cloak,* seem like incest. An almost childlike sense of connectedness encases Kate O'Brien's Ireland, so that any sorts of love her heroines choose fail to replace the love of family. In her last novels, as age removes the writer farthest from her own family, Kate O'Brien pictures that love less ambivalently than in her earlier novels, and its loss, though inevitable, is all the more poignant.

Thus, Kate O'Brien writes from a tragic perspective. If some of her heroines find a measure of contentment, within the family or without, none find enduring fulfilment. Despite its beguilement, family love strangles; love outside the family disappoints. The passion that Mary Lavelle experiences in Spain is too ephemeral to resist her Irish Catholic values; the romance that the young French woman Angèle Maury, in *The Last of Summer,* finds in Ireland is an incestuous fantasy; the love that Clare Halvey, in *As Music and Splendour,* discovers in Italy is an artistic myth.

Kate O'Brien's view of human relationships has profound implications for the artist. Her only choice is solitude, a severing, like Stephen Dedalus's, from nation and family. In several of her novels, explicitly in *Pray for the Wanderer* and *As Music and Splendour,* implicitly in *The Land of Spices,* Kate O'Brien denies the artist the pleasures of familial involvement so that she can be free to pursue her art. All her novels, however, tell a single tale: one writer's struggle to flee the forces that would crush her gifts and impede her self-expression. The artist's journey that begins in Kate O'Brien's fictionalised Limerick, in the bosom of a family, ends in exile as a solitary lesbian plies her craft.

When the Irish Censorship Board banned two of her books, Kate O'Brien learned, first hand, that the artist's need for freedom might generate political as well as personal discord, and she began to explore the texture of Irish life in terms of the issues of her day. Although she sympathises with Irish nationalism, Kate O'Brien decries its myopia and the isolationism and neutrality it produces amid rampaging tyranny. Her imaginative foci reach outward from her own anxieties as a woman and writer to Ireland and its place in the European community. In *That Lady,* for example, she transforms a woman's right to control her private life into a symbol of the liberation of the artist, of a nation, and finally of an entire continent.

If not actually autobiographical, Kate O'Brien's novels appear intensely personal, but the appearance is hard to confirm. An inordinately private person, she has left public few details about her life — no autobiography, no diaries or letters that might confirm what her novels suggest. Although we have an outline of her youth and young adulthood,[5] we have little available information about her maturity and the years after her brief marriage. We know so little, in fact, about Kate O'Brien's maturity that the temptation to seek her out in her fiction is almost irresistible. Her final published work, *Presentation Parlour,* bolsters a biographical interpretation of her novels. Evoking reminiscences of the aunts who offered 'authority, fun, advice, affection'[6] to their late sister's children, this memoir discloses how much of the ambience and detail in her novels come from her early years and affirm the influence of her Limerick youth. All of Kate O'Brien's novels are populated by characters and promulgated by events that figured in her life. Bits and pieces of poetry and music, such as the scary song Anna Murphy's father sings in *The Land of Spices,* are fragments of Kate O'Brien's childhood. So many details in her novels have their roots in her past that *Presentation Parlour* seems to give the reader licence to recognise the author in her adult characters and creations as well.

The exploration of character is far more important to Kate O'Brien than plot and action, and her elegant nuances of personality frequently blur the distinction between the author and her heroines. Her traditional literary style, far more akin to that of the Victorian novel than that of contemporary *avant-garde* fiction, contributes to our sense of her subjectivity. Writing in the third person and in the past tense, Kate O'Brien gives her omniscient narrator access to the thoughts and feelings of all her characters. Her technique permits so much authorial interjection that Vivian Mercier once remarked that a 'meditativeness colours her style too much'; she 'supplies her own commentary in and out of season'.[7] Other reviewers also pointed to Kate O'Brien's authorial presence. In *The Spectator,* for example, the reviewer of *The Land of Spices* observed, 'Miss O'Brien always follows the method of telling us about her characters rather than leaving them to express themselves in speech and action, and the danger of that method is that the character is bounded by the author's explanation.'[8] Such comments are fitting, for Kate O'Brien's characters speak in their own voices only when they speak to each other. Otherwise, the narrator speaks for all, commenting, interpreting, explaining, psychologising. This closeness between narrator and character also creates an intimacy between author and reader, so that each of Kate O'Brien's works seems a mirror to her inner and outer experience. We see her reflection on the pages of each of her novels.

In a short monograph, *English Diaries and Journals,* one of the few non-fiction prose works she left, Kate O'Brien addresses indirectly the subjectivity of her novels. The 'best and most typical English diarists would probably have been bores if they had not kept diaries',[9] she insists, and women would not have been diarists at all had they been able to be more 'directly self-expressive'. Writers like Dorothy Wordsworth and Fanny Burney, she says, were diarists only by default — *'faute de mieux'* (48); they wrote diaries only because they were unable to devote themselves exclusively to the writing of great novels. Kate O'Brien suggests that she gave herself over to the writing of fiction to achieve a more powerful mode of self-expression than the private diary could ever provide.

Kate O'Brien appears to her reader as a writer of relentless self-examination and psychological awareness, courageous in her willingness both to accept and surmount human weakness and in her unwillingness to adopt easy, conventional solutions. Her novels insist that personal strength and self-denial will succeed in the confrontation with human desire. But if Kate O'Brien concentrates on internal battles in her fiction, she also attends to her character's social and political *mise-en-scènes*. For all their attention to personal crises, Kate O'Brien's novels are acutely attuned to the issues of her day. Unlike many of her characters, the author felt deeply the plights of the less fortunate, and of Ireland and the nations of Europe, and she hoped for promising global remedies. She was connected to Ireland and to Europe not only by political sentiment, however, but by her abiding love of their history, literature, and music. The Spanish landscape, Italian opera, Renaissance art, and Irish nationalism spoke equally to her intellect and emotions. Finding Kate O'Brien in her fiction, we find a writer coming to terms with the small world she left and the larger world she chose, both as an Irish woman and an Irish writer.

No single methodology informs this study. Although all of Kate O'Brien's novels share basic themes and together seem to have a unity of purpose, each is distinctive, and each has dictated its most appropriate critical approach. *Without My Cloak* and *The Ante-Room* are considered primarily in terms of Irish social structure and cultural and religious conventions; *Pray for the Wanderer* is contextualised within the political and cultural history of contemporay Ireland. *The Land of Spices* calls for a comparison with James Joyce's *Portrait of the Artist as a Young Man,* while its successor, *The Last of Summer,* demands a psycho-historical reading. *Mary Lavelle* and *That Lady* are interpreted in relation to their Spanish setting: one to that nation's threatened freedom, the other to the novel's legendary Spanish source. *The Flower of May* and *As Music and Splendour* insist on placement within the genre, now open to public examination, of lesbian literature. All of Kate O'Brien's novels, however, assert loudly the need of women and writers for aesthetic, emotional, and sexual freedom.

Chronology

1897   Kate O'Brien born in Limerick on 3 December to Thomas and Catherine 'Katty' Thornhill O'Brien.

1902   Death of Catherine O'Brien. Kate O'Brien becomes the youngest boarder at Laurel Hill, a French convent school in Limerick.

1916   Thomas O'Brien dies. Kate O'Brien wins scholarship to study Arts at University College, Dublin.

1919   Receives her B.A. degree.

1920   Moves to England. Works as a free-lance journalist and then for the foreign language department of *The Manchester Guardian*.

1921   Teaches for the first half year at St. Mary's Convent, Hampstead. In the autumn visits the United States with her sister and brother-in-law.

1922   Spends ten months as a governess in Bilbao, Spain, for the Areilza family.

1923   Returns to London and marries Gustaaf Renier, a Dutch journalist. Marriage ends after eleven months.

1926   Play *Distinguished Villa* performed in London on 2 May at the Aldwych Theatre to wide acclaim.

1927   Writes several other plays, *The Silver Roan, Set in Platinum,* and *The Bridge,* which was produced in London at the Theatre Arts Club on 31 May.

1932   Her first novel, *Without My Cloak,* published by Heinemann, which handled all publication of her subsequent novels in England, and by Doubleday, which published all American editions of her novels except the final two. *Without My Cloak* awarded the James Tait Black Memorial Prize and the Hawthornden Prize.

1934   Publishes *The Ante-Room,* her second novel.

1936   Publishes her third novel, *Mary Lavelle,* which is banned in Ireland by the Censorship of Publications Board. *The Ante-Room* adapted unsuccessfully for the stage in London at the Queen's Theatre, 14 August.

1937   Inspired by the Spanish Civil War, publishes a travelogue, *Farewell, Spain,* that is banned in Franco's Spain. Kate O'Brien, herself, forbidden entry into Spain. *The Schoolroom Window* performed in London at Manuscript Theatre Club on 2 February.

1938   *Pray for the Wanderer,* her fourth novel, published.

1939-40   Lives in Oxford and London. Works for British Ministry of Information; writes *The Land of Spices.*

1941   *The Land of Spices,* fifth novel, published and banned in Ireland by the Censorship of Publications Board.

1942   Moves to Devon as a paying guest in the house of the novelist E.M. Delafield and writes *The Last of Summer.*

1943   *The Last of Summer,* sixth novel, published. *English Diaries and Journals* published.

1944   *The Last of Summer* produced as a play at the Phoenix Theatre, London, 8 June.

1945   Dublin premiere of *The Last of Summer* at the Gaiety Theatre, 16 July.

1946   Her seventh novel, *That Lady,* published.

1947   Elected to Irish Academy of Letters.

1949   Visits United States where *That Lady* is produced as a play in New York, at the Martin Beck Theatre, 22 November. *That Lady* published as a play.

1950   Returns to Ireland to live in Roundstone, Co. Galway.

1951   Biographical sketch, *Teresa of Avila,* published. Dublin premiere of *That Lady* at the Gaiety Theatre, 11 June.

1953   Eighth novel, *The Flower of May,* published.

1954   Lives in Rome, preparing for her ninth novel, *As Music and Splendour.*

1955   *For One Sweet Grape* made into a motion picture.

1957   Regains permission to enter Spain.

1958   *As Music and Splendour,* final novel, published. In April Irish premiere of *The Ante-Room* in the Dagg Hall of the Royal Irish Academy of Music.

1960   Returns again to England to live.

1962   Second travel book, *My Ireland,* published.

1963   *Presentation Parlour,* collection of family reminiscences, published.

1974   While working on her *Memoirs* and her tenth novel, *Constancy,* Kate O'Brien dies in Faversham, Kent on 13 August.

One
Biographical Sketch

A mantle of silence enshrouds the details of Kate O'Brien's adult life. Although she tells of her childhood years in her memoir *Presentation Parlour,* and travelogue *My Ireland,* Kate O'Brien has left only her fiction to indicate her central concerns and major preoccupations. Her mature life remains the subject of speculation.

Those who could tell us more about this distinctive presence in Irish letters have chosen, instead, to participate in her reticence. Perhaps to comply with her friend's wish for privacy, Lorna Reynolds, in *Kate O'Brien: A Literary Portrait* — and the only written portrait — delineates little of Kate O'Brien's person or personality as do the few critical essays devoted to her writings. Kate O'Brien has left scant clues — other than her fiction — to her thoughts and experiences as a woman and as a writer.

Her novels suggest that biographers, critics, friends, family, and the author alike are all reluctant to confront clandestine liaisons she may have enjoyed or an alternative sexual preference she may have satisfied. As a consequence, nearly all details of the writer's maturity, many of which could enrich the study of her novels, remain unknown and undocumented. Certainly, issues of sexual preference and practice are not, by definition, crucial to any literary study, but as Kate O'Brien moves them ever closer to the centre of her works, she becomes increasingly frank and impassioned in her depiction of the creative woman's search for autonomy. This analysis attempts to deal more directly than any of its predecessors with the issue of sexual preference, but its focus is literary, not biographical. Indeed, until the logical sources of biographical information are opened to public inquiry, Kate O'Brien's life story remains regrettably incomplete.

Kate O'Brien was born in Limerick, in 1897, to Thomas and Catherine 'Katty' Thornhill O'Brien, seventh in a family of four girls (of whom she was the youngest) and five boys. A successful breeder of hunter and harness thoroughbred horses, Thomas O'Brien provided his children with a life of loving and abundant comfort: education at the best neighbourhood schools, summers by the seashore, wardrobes full of current fashion, and the attention of devoted servants. But in 1902, life at Boru House, their large, brick home, was painfully disrupted when the young Katty O'Brien died of cancer. Five-year-old Kate was sent as the youngest boarder to Laurel Hill, the French convent school that her sisters attended.

A gifted student and favoured pupil, Kate O'Brien remained happily at Laurel Hill until 1916, when she entered University College, Dublin, to read English and French for her B.A. With her father's death the same year, the family's finances deteriorated, and she set about providing for her own education by winning a County Council scholarship, and, subsequently, her livelihood in England, as a free-lance journalist, a translator for the Foreign News page of the *Manchester Guardian*, and a teacher for half a year at a girls' school in Hampstead.

A veritable nomad, she spent several months of 1921 in Washington, D.C., with her sister and brother-in-law, the co-ordinator of de Valera's Bonds Drive in the United States. For ten months of 1922, she worked as a governess in a town outside Bilbao, Spain, teaching English to the two children of the Areilza family. Her young male charge, José, discovered her novels later in his life and wrote to her of his admiration for her work, particularly for *Mary Lavelle,* and of the fond memories it evoked. Recognising something of his own family, its social position, politics, and aspirations in Kate O'Brien's portrait of the Areavagas, he explained that he, like the novel's central character, had gone into politics, narrowly escaped death during the civil war, been appointed Mayor of Bilbao, become an under-secretary in the government and finally ambassador to Buenos Aires.[1] His letter suggests how deftly Kate O'Brien wove her personal experience of the Areilza family life into the art of *Mary Lavelle.*

Her marriage in 1923 in London to Gustaaf Renier, a Dutch journalist, lasted for less than a year, after which Kate O'Brien worked as a secretary and as an editor. She began her thirty-year career as a writer in 1926 with the play *Distinguished Villa,* the result of a wager with an old friend from Dublin that she could not write a play in a month. The play opened at the Aldwych Theatre in London on 2 May to wide acclaim. Kate O'Brien was especially pleased to receive a telegram from Sean O'Casey that read, 'Dublin ventures to congratulate Limerick'.[2]

Believing she had found her *metier,* Kate O'Brien continued to write plays: *The Silver Roan, Set in Platinum,* and *The Bridge,* which latter was produced at the Theatre Arts Club in London on 1 June 1927. But soon after this, at the urging of her agent and enjoying the relative solitude of a cottage near Tunbridge Wells, Kate O'Brien gave herself over to the writing of novels. Her first, *Without My Cloak,* was a family chronicle published by Heinemann in 1931 and awarded the Hawthornden and the James Tait Black Memorial Prizes. This was followed in 1934 by a sequel, *The Ante-Room,* and in 1936 by *Mary Lavelle. Mary Lavelle* was the first of two of Kate O'Brien's novels to be banned in Ireland by the Censorship of Publications Board.

Kate O'Brien responded to this censorship with pain and rage, and in her next novel, *Pray for the Wanderer* (1938), the thinly disguised author answers with vigour and vitriol. The failure of the stage adaption of *The Ante-Room* surely compounded her dismay over the reception of *Mary Lavelle* in Ireland. Perhaps as a result of these disappointments, Kate O'Brien moved away from fiction in her next piece of writing. Inspired by the conflicts leading to the Spanish Civil War, she wrote the highly personal travelogue, *Farewell, Spain,* a book so anti-Fascist that Franco banned it and its author from Spain.

Kate O'Brien spent the early years of World War II in London and Oxford working for the British Ministry of Information and completing her fifth novel, *The Land of Spices.* The single sentence describing the central character's discovery of her father and a male student 'in the embrace of love' persuaded the Irish Censorship Board to ban this novel, too, as 'in general tendency indecent and obscene'. In *The Last of Summer,* the novel she completed in 1943, at the Devon home of the writer E.M. Delafield, Kate O'Brien responded with even greater rancour; *The Last of Summer* is, perhaps, her most ferocious attack on her native land.

Her seventh novel, *That Lady* (1946) is, at least in part, Kate O'Brien's response to the savagery of World War II. Witnessing the devastation of a continent, Kate O'Brien expressed her horror in the way she knew best — demonstrating the toll that tyranny takes on an individual soul. Although set in sixteenth-century Spain, the novel's portrait of Philip II so displeased Franco that he denied Kate O'Brien entry into Spain when she tried once again to return in 1947. Finally, in 1957, the Irish Ambassador intervened on her behalf, enabling her once again to enter her surrogate homeland.[3]

Published in North America as *For One Sweet Grape, That Lady* was a critical and popular success. Director Guthrie McClintic and his wife, the actress Katherine Cornell, persuaded Kate O'Brien to transform the novel into a play and on 22 November 1949, *That Lady,* starring Katherine Cornell as Ana de Mendoza, opened in Broadway's Martin Beck Theatre with Kate O'Brien watching from the audience. It ran long enough that, with royalties reaped from the play, Kate O'Brien bought and moved into a house in Roundstone, County Galway, in 1950.

In 1951, Kate O'Brien published her biographical sketch *Teresa of Avila,* and in 1953, her penultimate novel, *The Flower of May.* She spent the early months of 1954 in Italy in preparation for what was to be her final novel, *As Music and Splendour.*[4] She studied and listened to opera, learning its history and the history of its great singers and great houses. She published her scrupulously accurate and detailed novel in 1958.

Forced by finances, and probably her emotions and her art, as well, Kate O'Brien abandoned Roundstone for England in 1960, and moved to Boughton, near Faversham, in Kent. Although she published no more fiction, she did produce a travelogue *My Ireland* in 1962, and *Presentation Parlour,* a memoir of the aunts who raised her, in 1963. Occasionally, she contributed articles she titled 'Long Distance' to the *Irish Times.* She was Ireland's representative on the central committee of the *Comunita Europea degli Scrittori* for which she visited Italy frequently. In 1962 she travelled to Russia.[5]

Ten years after publishing her last substantive work, Kate O'Brien died on 13 August 1974, and was buried in Kent. At the time of her death, she is said to have been working on her *Memoirs* and on a novel she called *Constancy.*[6]

Two

Without My Cloak

Why didst thou promise such a beauteous day,
And make me travel forth without my cloak,
To let base clouds o'ertake me in my way,
Hiding thy bravery in their rotten smoke?
'Tis not enough that through the cloud thou break,
To dry the rain on my storm-beaten face,
For no man well of such a salve can speak,
That heals the wound, and cures not the disgrace:
Nor can thy shame give physic to my grief;
Though thou repent, yet I have still the loss:
The offender's sorrow lends but weak relief
To him that bears the strong offence's cross,
    Ah! but those tears are pearl which thy love sheds,
    And they are rich, and ransom all ill deeds.

Sonnet xxxiv: William Shakespeare

Without My Cloak[1] is the first Irish novel to depict the wealthy Catholic merchant class that survived the Famine and continued to thrive in its aftermath. Kate O'Brien's first novel, published in 1931, introduces into twentieth-century Irish fiction a way of life and set of concerns that differ in the extreme from those depicted by her literary contemporaries. Preoccupied with the grave historical issues besetting Ireland, writers like Sean O'Faolain and Frank O'Connor emphasise the country's brutality and impoverishment. Bleak and depressing, their Ireland is a strife-torn, battle-scarred terrain. Kate O'Brien's preoccupation, however, is the merciless encroachment of social position and religion on emotions and human relations. In *Without My Cloak* she reconstructs the complacent society from which she came, whose inhabitants are untouched by social and political upheaval. She dissects the effects of Irish middle-class convention, bourgeois ideology, and Catholic belief on lives joined by blood and loyalty.

Kate O'Brien writes of late nineteenth-century Catholic men of humble origins, who have, by their work and wits, made substantial fortunes and live like aristocrats. Lavish furnishings complement their townhouses and riverside homes, on the outskirts of Mellick, that rival in their grandeur small estates of the Ascendancy. Their wives wear splendid costumes and jewels; fine horses pull their elegant carriages. Their acquisitiveness invigorates Joseph Lee's comment that 'not other worldly values, but a very intense "this worldly" concern with social status characterised Catholic society' in the late 1800s.[2] Nevertheless, Kate O'Brien's characters observe their Catholicism strictly; their faith and social code govern their lives. So circumscribed, they dwell in splendid isolation from both the Protestant Ascendency and the Catholic peasantry, experiencing neither envy or fear of the one, nor concern or dismay for the other.

Kate O'Brien emphasises their privileged detachment by concentrating exclusively on the Considines, a large merchant family that represents the best breeding, the greatest comfort, and the highest style among the bourgeoisie. She excludes the Anglo-Irish gentry from *Without My Cloak* and displays only once, through the eyes of Denis, the youngest and most sensitive of the Considines, those other familiar faces of Irish fiction, the 'beggars, drunkards, idiots, tramps, tinkers, cripples . . . Rheumy and filthy-smelling old men, sharp-eyed wolfish children, lively-tongued women who suckled dirty babies at dirty breasts, the old crone with lupus-eaten face who seemed to live in the doorway of St. Anthony's Church', and she tells us firmly that their 'images did not pursue him to his natural haunts . . . a wide and changeful playground' (127). What Kate O'Brien omits from *Without My Cloak,* then, is as significant as what she admits. She forces us to see the Considines — even as she asks us to understand them — as blindly isolated from the larger world around them, as smug, unconcerned, and frighteningly apathetic.

Although she continues to attack middle-class conventionality as she did in *Distinguished Villa,* when Kate O'Brien changes her setting from England to Ireland, and shifts from the play's polemic dialogue to the novel's rich descriptiveness, she equivocates. In *Without My Cloak* Kate O'Brien sympathises with the Considines as she satirises them in loving but ambivalent detail. She ridicules their pettiness, their contemptuousness, and their materialism; she denounces their possessiveness and their all-consuming loves; and she quietly scathes their moral and social codes that doom women to loveless marriages, to too many pregnancies, to emigration, to death. National events will soon batter down their doors, and Kate O'Brien approves, but she also savours the world those doors enclose. Despite its inadequacies, the family in *Without My Cloak* is not yet forced to face its demise or even the decline of its power. At the start of her fictional career, Kate O'Brien presents and preserves the world that gave rise to her fiction. Unified, intact, it keeps its members in its midst, but not for long.

In the dual plots of the unhappily married Caroline and her nephew

Denis, Kate O'Brien kindles the sparks of rebellion that will grow in her later novels into full-fledged personal revolt. Thus, in *Without My Cloak,* Kate O'Brien creates a work that is both a *sotto voce* critique of the distinctive qualities of a social class and, at the same time, an affecting elegy for a lost way of life. By irony and omission, she suggests the troubling aspects and dark corners of privilege and piety — aspects never so troubling and corners never so dark, though, that she would remove her characters from the shelter of their parlours.

Kate O'Brien's choice of Shakespeare's 'Sonnet Thirty-four' as an epigraph to the novel and as the source for its title immediately bares her ambivalence. The speaker of the sonnet accuses his lover of exposing him, unprotected ('without my cloak'), to shame. Although the lover apologises and the speaker professes forgiveness, all is not well. Despite their avowed rapprochement, the speaker seems still to suffer, still to harbour a grievance. Their discord is repeated in the Considines' emotions. The sonnet's curious blending of offender and offended — both the speaker and his beloved are disgraced, both shed tears of shame — is recalled in Caroline's and Denis's relationships with their family. Who has hurt whom? Has Caroline defamed the family, or has it betrayed her by dragging her back to Mellick? The novel's closing promise of love echoes the sonnet's closing promise of forgiveness, self-deluded at best, cynical and dishonest at worst.

In calling attention to feelings of obligation, betrayal, and shame, 'Sonnet Thirty-four' emphasises the novel's social focus and highlights the degree to which society constrains the Considines. What makes *Without My Cloak* remarkable, however, is the absence of any fictional analogue in Irish literary tradition for what Kate O'Brien attempts, and indeed accomplishes, in her first novel. She may have found a paradigm in *The Forsyte Saga*,[3] John Galsworthy's distillation of Victorian middle-class society, published nine years earlier. *Without My Cloak* has far more in common with Galsworthy's family saga than with any Irish novel. *The Irish Times* was the first to cite the resemblance: Kate O'Brien's 'book cannot escape comparison with Mr. Galsworthy's annals of the English bourgeois family,' its critic wrote in the paper's review of *Without My Cloak*.[4] Vivian Mercier also notes the similarities between the works. In an early essay on Kate O'Brien's novels, he comments, '*Without My Cloak* sets out to be the *Forsyte Saga* of the upper middle-class in Limerick . . . but changes course before half way through'. Mercier sees the change as Kate O'Brien's realistic appraisal of the emotional life and behaviour of a nineteenth-century Irish Catholic matron.[5]

The plots and sub-plots of *The Forsyte Saga*, create two central and connected stories that reappear in Irish guise in *Without My Cloak* to demonstrate 'the impingement of Beauty and the claims of Freedom on a possessive world' (xiii). The first concerns Soames Forsyte, the prime example of possessive materialism that Galsworthy refers to as 'Forsyteism', and Irene, the 'concretion of disturbing beauty' (xii), who has married Soames without loving him. Soames refuses to divorce Irene. She is his; he is a Forsyte; and Forsytes do not relinquish their property. After Irene leaves him, risking social condemnation, Soames tries first to repossess her and then to divorce her so that he can remarry and produce an heir.

The second plot revolves around the family patriarch, Old Jolyon Forsyte, and the conversion of his lineage from Forsyteism to the worship of Beauty. In Old Jolyon and his son Young Jolyon, the Forsyte strain has begun to decay; sentiment has eroded their materialism. Irene's marriage to Young Jolyon produces Jon, the antithesis of the Forsytes, an imaginative, creative spirit who appreciates beauty for its own sake. The old conflict between beauty and Forsyteism is renewed when Jon and Soames's daughter, Fleur, fall in love. But the more Fleur reveals the traits of her lineage, the more Jon becomes disenchanted. Repudiating Fleur, he confirms the Forsytes' demise.

In many respects, to know the Forsytes is to know the Considines. Honest John Considine's loving patriarchal leadership recalls Old Jolyon Forsyte's paternalism toward Young Jolyon and his children; Anthony's excessive love for Denis recalls Soames's possessive love of Fleur; Theresa Considine's marriage to the feckless Danny Mulqueen recalls Winifred Forsyte's marriage to the wastrel Montague Dartie; competition among the Considine siblings recalls the constant vying for social superiority among the Forsytes. But most compelling and most precisely, the struggles of Caroline Lanigan and Denis Considine against their environment recall those of Irene and Jon Forsyte.

The similarities between Kate O'Brien's characters and the Forsytes establish their social type; the differences between them highlight the idiosyncrasies of bourgeois life in Ireland. The Considines mirror their English counterparts in social position, conventional tastes, and conservative politics, but they differ from them profoundly in the way their Catholicism circumscribes their lives. If, like Galsworthy, Kate O'Brien derides the materialism and social pretensions of the Considines, she treats their spirituality with less irony. To be sure, she occasionally satirises their religiosity, but empathy and compassion mark this dimension of her portraits more frequently than others.

Based on Kate O'Brien's family annals, the history of the Considines is an Irish version of the Forsytes'. Both families choose to hide their modest beginnings. Mentioned only rarely, and never in public, the first Anthony Considine came to Mellick from the west of Ireland, penniless, married the first woman he spoke to in the town, and was killed in a brawl eleven months later on the night his son, John Anthony, was born. That son, Honest John, is the prototype of the late nineteenth-century Irish businessman whose ambition has earned him position and power. Once a 'barefoot nobody' working in his mother's crubeen shop, he now enjoys a respectable old age as 'the most extensive forage dealer and exporter in Ireland and one of the wealthiest men in the south' (16), well able to provide for his twenty-five grandchildren. Two of his children — a doctor and a priest — typify the desire of his class 'to move out of business as soon as means became available to acquire status in more socially respected occupations'.[6] Only his two youngest, and cleverest, sons work with him. His daughter Caroline has married a successful lawyer.

Honest John revels in his hard-won respectability and possessions — particularly in his townhouse furnished with leather and mahogany, Waterford crystal, and old Dublin silver. His son Anthony, having inherited Honest John's business acumen, audacity, and 'unexplainable flair for buying at the right moment' (107), is destined also to inherit his father's place at Considine and Company. As a testament to his prestige, Anthony builds River Hill, a large home outside of town, not unlike Soames's country 'palace' (59). River Hill, Honest John teases, seems 'a country mansion more suited to a duke than a forage merchant' (12). What Anthony 'wanted in his house, as in other things, was the best that his epoch could give him' (22). Not only Honest John, but the narrator as well, pricks Anthony's pretentiousness here, commenting that 'the best that 1860 could give him in domestic architecture was not felicitous . . . but [Anthony] built consciously for his posterity and so it is necessary to consider the house from posterity's angle' (22). Future eyes would judge Anthony's 'high-class up-to-date gentleman's residence' a 'crude . . . mansion' (23-4).

Like the Forsytes, the Considines amass their fortunes with thought of little else. Honest John worries about the 'Potato Blight', as he tellingly understates it, chiefly because 'it was disastrous to his trade' (15). Kate O'Brien treats his commercial self-absorption with a touch of humour when she tells us that he greeted the American Civil War

with callous pleasure, foreseeing that American trade would not ride the seas very well while it lasted . . . He was entirely cynical about the principles of the war. When his daughters told him that slavery was a shocking thing and that Pio Nono had declared against the Confederates, he said, 'Quite right, my little girl; a scandalous state of affairs', and went on eating bread and jam in deep contentment. (107)

But humour wanes when Kate O'Brien asks us to consider such a narrow view from 'posterity's angle' as well. Following the social upheavals of the summer of 1870 month by month, she ruthlessly juxtaposes the Considines' provincial concerns with global events. She ridicules the complacency that permits them to live largely unaffected, except when they can profit by the misfortunes of others:

The Summer of 1870 was eventful and alarming for the world. For the Considines it blossomed with warm, fulfilling peace. In June Charles Dickens died and Millicent's betrothal to Gerard Hennessy was announced. In July France and Prussia went to war and Anthony made a brilliant deal with North Sea ports to supply forage to the Prussian Army. In August guns growled over Paris, and Mr. Gladstone got his Irish Land Bill through. Victor Considine came of age that month and there was a brilliant dance in Finlay Square at which all the Hennessys attended. In September Sedan, Eugénie's flight, the Marseillaise — in September too, Millicent's marriage at St. Peter's with a hundred guests and three hundred wedding presents, bridesmaids and Mellick lace, rice, silver slippers and orange blossom, a honeymoon among the English Lakes. (206)

While they are not totally removed from their country's affairs, the Considines consider national issues according to one of the foremost dictates of Forsyteism: acknowledge politics only insofar as politics encroaches on one's assets and property. Honest John scorns the nationalist agitators, Young Irelanders and Ribbonmen, who threaten the orderly flow of commerce. Indeed, he eschews all politics, having had only one enthusiasm: Daniel O'Connell, the 'Liberator', as he unfailingly called him, who was staunchly supported by Irish mercantile interests for his advocacy of constitutional nationalism and repudiation of violence. After O'Connell's death, Honest John disregarded his country's affairs almost completely. To his children, politics are like 'firearms — things that shouldn't be left about the house' (44). A timid nationalist like his father, Anthony has no sympathy with political agitators and no 'patience with the crazy dream that seemed to be forever rising up from Ireland to enshroud her' (119). As much as commerce permits, he ignores Fenian and agrarian disturbances. Anthony does have sufficient pride as a Catholic and an Irishman, however, to refuse to join the Protestant landowners and merchants with whom he trades in vilifying his disruptive countrymen. Confronted with the national and class biases of the Anglo-Irish, he cannot abandon his Catholic compatriots completely. At moments such as these, Irish Catholic instincts overwhelm mercantile interests.

But sympathy for social inferiors, Irishmen or not, disappears when Anthony's business seems threatened. He has no tolerance for his workers' attempts to unionise. Their single, fleeting appearance in the novel mirrors the Considines' arrogant disregard for the 'wounds of the world' (271). 'Contemptuous' of their employees, Anthony's father and grandfather had set an example for Mellick's merchants by remaining 'tranquil[ly] indifferent' (268) to any such efforts. Anthony moves beyond his forebears' disregard and becomes a hero among Mellick's employers when he fires four dockers for protesting against the dismissal of one of their fellows:

The idea that anyone, least of all a few illiterate hooligans, should attempt to tell an employer when to sack or when not to sack his employees, or to say what they should be paid or for what hours they should work, was simply an insane conception, in Anthony's view. (270-71)

Among the Considines, only Denis understands the 'pathos and significance', the 'tragic dignity' of the 'four dirty men', the human urgency of their protest and the range of its political implications. Distressed by his father's 'imperious, picturesque, theatrical, cheap' (272) response, Denis asserts their right to form trade unions. He defends them as he might defend himself against Anthony's possessiveness, saying, 'They're free souls, after all' (274). Denis is Kate O'Brien's portent of change.

Like Galsworthy, Kate O'Brien cites the limitations of the bourgeoisie in realms other than nation and class. Pettiness and snobbery characterise the daily agendas of the Considines. When Molly Considine, Anthony's wife, must move from King's Crescent to River Hill, her attitude is typical:

She had been happy in King's Crescent, because, as she said, its houses were among the best in the town, and residence in them gave definite prestige. She had liked her snobbish neighbours, had liked the nods and becks of genteel town life, the tattle and the tea-drinking, the pretty posing to and fro in her carriage, the flattery that twittered unceasingly about her frou-frou elegance, and the envy that derided it. (26)

The imagery and excessive alliteration here — the tattle and tea-drinking of town life, the flattery of her frou-frou elegance — renders Molly's snobbish perspective as little more than child-like silliness. But Kate O'Brien indicates that Considine snobbery can take a far more virulent form in the family's attitude towards the peasant girl Christina, Denis's lover, whose beauty, bastardy, and simple class conceal her father's aristocratic status. To Anthony, whose love for Denis disposes him to accept Christina, she is still 'a scullery maid, the bastard of a scullery maid — stupid, quiet, unremarkable . . . the usual helpless cargo of the emigrant ship' (366). That 'there wasn't a man or woman in Glenwilliam that hadn't a good word for the quiet, good-looking girl' (293) is of little import where social inferiors maintain class distinctions with the vigilance of the bourgeoisie. 'Illegitimate and without a half-penny of a fortune, [Christina's] chances of marriage among the small, respectable farmers round about were non-existent. . . . The effort [to make such a match] would have been regarded as comic throughout the baronies' (293).

Considine women belong to their men, and Denis's family deems him entitled to a finer possession. Both Kate O'Brien and Galsworthy condemn the Victorian sense of property that treats women as chattels. Even the pitiable Jim Lanigan is 'dumbly happy in the possession' (86) of his wife, Caroline, and accepts the common delusion that her discontent is insignificant. The far more affectionate Anthony constantly calls Molly 'my girl', 'my little girl' (28). 'He led and his wife followed. It never occurred to him that she should not, or that there was anything else for her to do; he had not loved her quite enough for that' (31).

Among the Considines, marriage, like one's house and carriage, is a measure of prestige, and therefore the external impression it makes matters more than the feelings it embodies. When Caroline Lanigan cries out to her brother Eddy from the pain of her marital deprivation, he answers in cynical consolation, 'Look at the world! Why, almost everyone is putting up with marriage somehow, without what you call love!' (58). Eddy's cynicism may stem, in part, from his own unrequited feeling for Caroline that has forced him to live a loveless, though not thoroughly unsatisfying, existence outside Mellick. But Caroline hears Eddy's comment as the voice of their shared world, 'tarred with the . . . brush of respectability' (58) — that insists she do her duty, love or not. Mellick and the Considine ethos insist that she is best 'off here . . . children, after all, and security, and an appointed place — and all this lovely countryside about you — if it isn't a perfect life, oh, it's still a pretty good one' (56).

Children, too, are possessions. The need to possess his son tarnishes Anthony's love for Denis, which exceeds even his love for Molly. Denis is 'a prisoner' (438) of his father's devotion, and although Denis returns that love, Kate O'Brien likens it to 'chain dropped softly on chain' (436), a 'heavy shroud' that 'possessed and smothered him' (394). Anthony cannot see that his 'absorbing passion' is 'cruelly immoral . . . dangerous or unnatural' (238). After Molly dies, he eschews remarriage and instead indulges Denis so as 'to make himself indispensable and . . . that familiar, traditional life that might have seemed a prison the only possible life because he was the centre of it' (238). Denis cannot fend off the malignant aspects of his father's love, nor can he, like Jon Forsyte, escape. 'Oh God', he cries, 'We own one another here! Body and soul — do we possess one another for ever, us Considines? What in hell's the matter with us, that we insist on owning things' (434-5), on owning each other? Denis's anguish is a poignant outcry against a society in which custody figures in even the most intimate relationships.

But as Kate O'Brien implies similarities between the English and Irish bourgeoisie, she also indicates Mellick's distinctiveness. Irene Forsyte rebelled against the 'Victorian ideal' (611) and, despite the disgrace of divorce, transgresses the conventions of her day to find her freedom. No such path is open to Caroline. The religious and social codes of their small Irish city determine the Considines' destinies, ensure their entrapment and preclude their personal freedom. As Caroline and Denis try to resolve their problems, their moral code asserts itself, and family life oppresses them. In Kate O'Brien's view, they have no way out. Caroline may flee to London, but only briefly, for even in flight, she imagines her return: 'Where could you hide in Mellick from a loving husband?' (148). She falls in love with Richard Froude, a Protestant Londoner, and yet she submits when Anthony, whose wrath is typical of the Considines, comes to retrieve her. Anthony cannot set his 'Sister Caroline above his surname' (159), and neither can Caroline see herself as anything but a Considine. She shares with her family the horror of gossip, the 'cheap and spiteful bandying of the Considine name' (164), the gloating of the town at a wife who leaves her husband for 'nothing at all'. She is the twenty years of her marriage to Jim. She has no other identity. Her 'sex and training and tradition' have made her 'a creature of her Church and of her filial and maternal and herd instincts, a piece of her own setting' (193). As Eddy wryly explains to her, she is 'very nicely hedged about, thank heaven' (57).

Kate O'Brien stresses the religious aspect of Caroline's captivity. Richard Froude cannot understand her belief in marriage as a sacrament or her conviction that the union between husband and wife is not a personal matter, but God's will. The belief in mortal sin that drives her from him strikes her lover as 'nonsense' (192). But the imagery with which Kate O'Brien describes Caroline's unhappiness conveys the power of her Catholicism. Tears drop from her eyes 'as close together as beads in a decade of the rosary' (142). Reciting a litany of family ties and constraints, Caroline appears 'with a glitter as of votive candles over her face and the starred blue wisp of sky behind her . . . [like] the Queen of Sorrows in a Shrine' (178). As the lovers are about to part, Caroline watches as Richard lights 'six candles on the mantelpiece and . . . [thinks] of the acolytes in the Jesuit Church at Mellick preparing the High Altar for Benediction' (195). Kate O'Brien writes with no irony here; empathy pervades her treatment of the mythology that underlies the Considine way of life, their system of belief that runs deeper than their worship of possessions and their hauteur. The Church both controls this family and sustains it.

Unable to bridge the gap between his upper-class English background and her bourgeois Irish Catholic ethics, Richard and Caroline are alien to each other. A 'stranger to mortal sin and to the Catholic mind' (194), he cannot grasp that, unawakened sexually and with her soul at stake, she cannot leave the past she knows for a future she can only surmise. Kate O'Brien insists that, had Richard's scruples allowed him to make love with her, Caroline would have left Mellick and 'Jim-and-the-children' (172), would have been 'transfigured out of all [her] setting' (193). 'A mortal sin could have secured' (194) her for Richard, but 'a sentimentalist according to his day', he wants Caroline 'for ever', and so it seems to him that 'he must not take her now' (190). Richard's gallantry evokes 'the ghosts' that chain Caroline 'back in her own place where wives are faithful' (196). Both Caroline and Richard are irrevocably entrapped in their social codes, she in her Irish Catholicism, he in his Victorian sensibility.

Kate O'Brien has painted Richard with a pale palette. We know little about him — who he really is, what he thinks, or what he feels — except for the background and values that lead to his losing Caroline. Richard is hardly more than an idea, a metaphoric construction representing the possibility of Caroline's escape, the incarnation of a deliverance she dares not risk. He is a function of the author's inability or unwillingness to assert that an Irishwoman such as Caroline, so thoroughly confined, can ever extricate herself. Richard is the first among Kate O'Brien's male characters to embody her conviction that romantic passion must inevitably succumb to familial authority. Had the author fashioned him along the lines of Anthony Considine, a man whose devotion to family is unmistakable, whose love for wife and son is undeniable, Caroline might have escaped. But Kate O'Brien apparently saw little hope of Caroline's moving beyond Mellick. Jim Lanigan, in his thin-lipped, straight-laced rigour and suppressed pain, is far more commanding, and, as a character, overwhelms Richard. Jim is Caroline's reality; Richard, only her promise, doomed to disappoint.

Dimly sensing the meaning of Richard's promise, Caroline is aware that her life is profoundly lacking, but she knows the body's power only in a negative sense. If her husband, Jim, had satisfied her sexual needs, Caroline would have cherished him, Kate O'Brien insists, loved him with liberated desire. The sexuality, repressed by Caroline, is expressed by Molly, who, in childbirth, sacrifices her life to her passion for Anthony, and by Christina, who, with nothing to lose but her soul, risks that loss in the physical demonstration of her love for Denis. The sexuality of Kate O'Brien's female characters is startling. So hostile was it to the Irish fictional norms of her day that, as expressed later in *Mary Lavelle,* it incurred the wrath of the Censorship Board. Even later, a single reference to male homosexuality caused *The Land of Spices* to be banned.

Kate O'Brien contrives no happy ending for Caroline, who returns to a sterile household, her passion and compassion gone. 'Love that Caroline had so long foregone, then found and flung aside and wept for, had now become a thing she hated to consider. It was only with mock-kindness that she looked on . . . legitimate pairs of young lovers' (372). And when she hears of Denis's adultery with Christina she loses all 'endurance'. A tale of that sort of love 'never reached her in gossip or novel or play, without encountering her cruel jibe. Only thus could she bear the disturbance which such news still made among nerves and desires that she wished to regard as dead' (372).

Caroline's disdain for sinful love like Denis and Christina's equals the Considines', but here, Kate O'Brien reveals that Caroline's intolerance is not simply the limited product of class snobbery and religious indoctrination. Rather, it has grown from her inability to make the leap that would remove her from Mellick. Caroline reflects Kate O'Brien's need to sympathise with the characters she exposes.

Kate O'Brien retells Caroline's story with some variation in the plot that surrounds Denis Considine: his father's obsession with him, his own love first for Christina, and later for Anna Hennessy. Denis belongs to the next generation of Considines, and he rebels more acutely, more consciously, against his family's values, most powerfully embodied in his father. He wishes to develop his sensitivity and artistry, to pursue beauty rather than business as his father and his grandfather have ordained. Anthony's possessive love hampers Denis's success; alternatives to his demands seem impossible. Denis both luxuriates in and resists this love, 'see-sawing for ever between resentment and adoration of his father'.

Only in rare moments of something like fury, when seized with an unreasonable idea that he was being treated as if he were a lunatic or a dangerous prisoner, he shouted savagely at Anthony: 'Leave me alone, father! Oh, God, go away and leave me alone!'

But as Anthony obeyed and left him Denis had almost always to run after him and catch his arm. For he could not endure to hurt this man, whom no one but he could really hurt. (430)

When Denis falls in love with Christina, the author tantalises us with the hope that she will be the means of his escape. Christina holds out the promise of romantic plots and fairy-tale endings of peasants transformed into princesses. But then Kate O'Brien jolts us with the reminder that as a member of the Irish upper middle class, Denis is just as unlikely to marry a bastard peasant girl as Caroline is to leave her husband and children. In their horror upon learning that Christina and Denis have been lovers, as when they heard of Caroline's flight, the Considines personify the obstacles confronting Mellick's deviants. If Kate O'Brien treats their response with humour and irony, she does not diminish its chilling effect on Denis:

...it was to be gathered that they were suffering severely from shock.

Sophia went into straightforward hysterics and swayed back and forth on her chair, giving out a staccato series of gasps and giggles.

Agnes's face was buried in her hands. She sobbed and prayed aloud with violence. That she should see such wickedness and live seemed like a miracle. In one hour sacrilege had been revealed to her — for was it not sacrilege to call a priest a frog? — and insolence to authority and, and — Agnes did not know how to name the most terrible sin of all. All these from one of her own blood, a boy of nineteen who dwelt in this very house with her! (371)

To the reader, the aunts' reaction seems absurd; to Denis it seems absolute moral and social authority. Even though Denis's affair is 'deplorable and a bitter disappointment' (376), Anthony tries to console his son. His face grows 'shadowy, his form gigantic, a gigantic priest he seemed to become... The room swam about Denis. He tumbled forward into Anthony's arms' (378). This gigantic priestly form, the combination of familial and ecclesiastical prohibition, accounts as much for the eventual ebbing of Denis's feeling for Christina as does any emotional tide and keeps Denis from Christina, just as it drives Caroline back to Mellick. The supremacy of religion is what distinguishes Kate O'Brien's bourgeois milieu from Galsworthy's.

Thus, as in her treatment of Caroline and Richard, Kate O'Brien delineates the religious as well as the social dimension of Denis and Christina's plight. Believing, like any well-trained Catholic, that she risks losing eternal bliss for transient joy, yet surprised to discover that she can commit mortal sin without feeling a trace of guilt, Christina gives herself to Denis with the catechism's 'perfect knowledge and full consent'. Denis, too, must answer to their mutual moral obligation: 'A word from Christina now, from that chaste, Catholic Christina, whose wish it was to serve God and be holy, would have brought Denis back, quick as an arrow, from his uncalculating passionate purpose' (308). But Christina withholds that word, and convinced that she is consigning her soul to damnation, she gives herself to Denis. Overwhelmed by the beauty of their physical passion, however, the lovers cannot imagine their souls blackened; briefly, they cast aside their belief in sin. Christina speaks for them both, 'How could God put the like of you in hell, my darling? Sure doesn't He love you more than I do?' (309). But the imagery with which Kate O'Brien introduces their lovemaking foreshadows its consequences and connotes the power of the injunctions against it. Denis sees Christina's 'arms open wide as if for crucifixion, and it seemed to him that he had to run to them from a long way off, across a perilous plain' (307-8). The Golgothan simile and 'perilous plain' anticipate Christina's martyrdom to the strictures of Mellick morality.

Father Tom, who is Denis's uncle and Christina's priest, discovers the pair kissing. Unaware that they have committed adultery, he is shocked by both their passion and the social indiscretion of a Considine holding a servant girl in his arms. Moved by moral outrage and Considine snobbery, he sends Christina to America. When he and the family learn that Denis and Christina have been lovers, however, Tom tells Denis where he can find Christina and marry her. Here, both Kate O'Brien's disappointment with, and esteem for, the world she depicts are apparent. When confronted with only a spiritual issue and not with family pride, Father Tom becomes a human and sympathetic, if still limited, representative of the family's morality. He had sent Christina off not solely in an act of cruelty, as Denis believed, but also as an act of charity, so far as he knew and understood charity. Had he known that the two had been lovers, he would have agonised over Christina, a 'fallen woman', rather than send her away. He would have busied himself with her soul's reclamation. 'He would have been kinder to the accomplished sinner because of his constitutional terror of [sin], than to what he saw merely as temptation and a dangerous slur on Considine pride' (373).

The family members as well worry over Christina and urge Denis to go after her. Their collective sense of decency causes them great pain. Looking away would have been easier and more dignified — Christina was, after all, thousands of miles from Mellick. But 'that a girl might be in trouble and maybe in danger of death at the other end of the world through the fault of one of them . . . was a risk their consciences could not accommodate' (374). They must accept her as one of themselves, endure the gossip of Mellick, and share in Denis's public disgrace. Kate O'Brien discards the satire with which she had earlier tainted the family's view of the lovers, and treats its moral concern as genuine, if misguided, compassion. If she faults the Considines for their excoriation, and if she condemns their banishing of Christina, Kate O'Brien applauds their wish to bring her back, to legitimise the relationship in the eyes of Mellick society.

Finding Christina, Denis also finds that his passion has been only physical; nevertheless, Considine virtue and Christina's goodness sustain his determination to marry her. From the beginning, however, Christina has known that they could never be happy, that she could never find peace in his world. She aptly assesses how the 'proud middle class' (320) would regard her:

> Beyond the first storms and the first piercing humiliations, she saw . . . that she would have to live at the centre of that great, possessive horde, unforgiven by them, unaccepted, but forever hemmed in; felt their contemptuous eyes on her as she fumbled to learn their superficial tricks . . . fumbled and failed because of them standing by; saw their resentment if she made Denis happy, their sagacious head-wagging if she didn't . . . (320-21)

She gives Denis what his family and his father can never give him — his freedom. Denis returns home to Anthony. 'God! If you knew how I missed you in America,' he murmured. Instantly tears glinted in Anthony's eyes. 'River Hill was a tomb without you, my son,' he said (428).

Having returned to Mellick, Denis again feels restive. He rebels once more, and on the eve of his twenty-first birthday, when he is to assume an influential place in the family business, he dishonours himself and the family by fleeing the Considine offices, terrified by the burden they imply. He decides to leave Mellick and satisfy his interest in landscape architecture. The novel might well have ended here, so strongly has Kate O'Brien suggested that, to find self-fulfilment, Denis, like Jon Forsyte, must leave his claustrophobic family. His Uncle Eddy, who straddles the wall between Mellick and the outside, warns him:

> If you live among Considines, making their life and interest yours, you'l do so out of unconvinced affection — your personality will be wounded, exasperated, and insulted even, every week of the year . . . The compromise that will be required of you in all your years in Mellick will be a long one . . . Mellick isn't your life . . . (245)

The pattern Kate O'Brien establishes for Denis in *Without My Cloak* traces the model of Jon Forsyte only so far, however. Jon left England to make a new life in Canada, but Kate O'Brien holds Denis back. Personifying the author's ambivalence towards the world she has replicated, the Considines appear malefic, worthy of rejection, yet too powerful for an individual to withstand. But they also have endearing, human qualities: despite their flaws — their pettiness, their destructive potential, their snobbery, their spite — none of them will ever desert the family.

Thus, on the eve of Denis's departure, as he lurks outside a dance in his honour at River Hill, he meets Anna Hennessy, a member of a family as patrician as his own and every inch their social peer. The description of Anna's grandfather, John Aloysius Hennessy, typifies, for a final time, the values that shape the novel's milieu:

he inherited a thin, proud blood, that had known power and pride in other centuries, and was tinged with their traditions . . . He stood for the autocracy of wealth and the supremacy of the bourgeoisie, but he was in spirit, faintly and deprecatorily as he might suggest it, an aristocrat. He cared little for distinctions of rank, which seemed to him to settle themselves arbitrarily in the womb, but he cared much for the tradition of fine behaviour and fine breeding in the Hennessys. He exacted a harsh standard of conduct from his dependents, not out of little but out of much understanding of life, being as fully aware of the rebellious hearts of men as he was convinced that it was necessary for them to conform to arbitrarily set conventions. (452)

As Honest John preferred Denis among his many grandchildren, so John Aloysius prefers Anna, unconventional, intellectual, independent, and beautiful. Denis knows one of his cousins plans to propose to Anna, but when he sees her in the garden, 'burning like a lost soul, like a poet or a saint or a sinner, like an unhappy soul in purgatory . . . a light set out in the jungle to hypnotise wild beasts' (462), he falls instantly in love. The similes Kate O'Brien uses to depict Anna equally describe Denis. Like Narcissus, he has fallen in love with his reflection; he has found his female likeness, his only appropriate mate. He abandons his plans to leave, and dancing with Anna into a room filled with family and friends, he makes clear to all assembled that they are each other's destiny.

Anna Hennessy is even less real than Richard Froude. The embodiment of the social and moral entities that keep Denis at home, she is a *dea ex machina*. If John Aloysius meant his offspring to conform to 'arbitrarily set conventions', Anna complies fully. She believes 'even more fantastically than [he] in the duty of the individual to submit himself to the rule of his tradition' (458). Denis must stay, she insists, must 'try to be happy with the same old cant' (466). By falling in love with Anna, Denis capitulates to all that he hoped to escape. 'The tradition, conformity, conservatism — they were values that were not his, they were pride and funny pomp and the will of others — but they were home, too, his history, and his guardians' (248). With Anna, Kate O'Brien suggests, Denis can make peace with his loving enemies and find a place among them; 'Would this do?' he heard himself asking Anthony, half in despair, half in hope. 'Could we settle it this way, father?' (466). Anna is Denis's great compromise. Accepting her, he accepts all that Mellick and the Considines represent. A sombre conclusion would confirm Kate O'Brien's stubborn insinuation that Denis can never be content at home. But as *Without My Cloak* ends, Anna, dressed in pure white, seems to glow. She appears before Denis as Asia, Shelley's 'Child of Light', about to be reunited with the unbound Prometheus, liberator of mankind from the tyranny of the gods. Exposing Anna's 'sensuousness, spirituality, and penetrative fire' (462), Kate O'Brien asks the reader to believe that, now, Denis will shed his cloak of confinement. The fire between the two engulfs the room, so that even the most unobservant witness recognises that they are 'lovers'. Together, transcendent, with a gravity echoing Shelley's heavenly dance, Denis and Anna move 'to a music of fate and death, and triumph and resignation' (469). Yet for all its brightness, the finale is shadowed. The lovers' waltz is a dance of 'death' and 'resignation' as well as of 'triumph' and 'fate'.

The final sentence is equally ominous: 'Anthony stared at his son; his brilliant eyes blazed love on him' (469). If Denis has become Anna's, he is all the more Anthony's; Anna has saved him for his family and for Mellick. No Prometheus, Denis will marry her, accepting his tradition and hers. The couple's dance before their gathered families is as much Denis's submission to the old gods as it is his victory over them.

Three

The Ante-Room

The Ante-Room,[1] Kate O'Brien's second novel, is set in 1880, three years after the conclusion of *Without My Cloak*. A sequel, in a sense, to the earlier work and published three years later, *The Ante-Room* is also set in Mellick, its bourgeois inhabitants also isolated by privilege from the civil unrest of even that eventful year. In this novel, however, Kate O'Brien suggests, more forcibly than in her first, that the prosperity that takes comfort for granted and the orthodox belief that preordains personal choice are imperilled. Omens are everywhere, though the characters fail to heed them, remaining instead behind the curtained windows of their homes and the stained-glass of their churches.

Class and creed are as important in *The Ante-Room* as in *Without My Cloak,* and although Kate O'Brien treats her subjects more romantically, engaging in little editorial irony, she continues to suggest the limitations of their Mellick environment. But in *The Ante-Room,* Kate O'Brien shifts her emphasis from social milieu to individual psyche. The mores, expectations, and beliefs that circumscribed the characters in *Without My Cloak* become in *The Ante-Room* the core of one woman's emotional anguish. Focusing particularly on the religious dimension of her characters', lives, the author now treats Irish Catholicism as an inner, psychological dynamic rather than an external, social force. Whereas Caroline Lanigan and Denis Considine moved according to the mandates of their Church, their family, and Mellick society, Agnes Mulqueen, the youngest daughter of one branch of the Considines, is guided only by her rigorous scruples. She struggles in secrecy to stifle her thoughts of love for Vincent O'Regan, her brother-in-law. Her inner battles predict what lies ahead for Kate O'Brien's other heroines. Agnes is the first to be distinguished by her need and capacity to act as *she* believes she should. Yet so strong is Agnes's morality, so organic is her relationship with her upbringing, that her choice accords fully with her Catholic training.

Here, as in her first novel, Kate O'Brien probes the forces that bind the individual to her origins. Together, these novels mourn a world whose dissolution Kate O'Brien knew was imminent and a way of life from which she had to flee. *The Ante-Room* is the last of her works in which the central character fails to sever her ties with family and country. Responding not to social pressure but to a sense of personal obligation, Agnes Mulqueen can no more betray her family, especially her sister Marie-Rose, than Caroline Lanigan or Denis Considine could have abandoned their family. In the autobiographical *Presentation Parlour,* describing the closeness between her aunts, and perhaps a feeling she experienced for her sisters, Kate O'Brien writes that the 'need to be within reach of one another' was 'more than a happiness'; it was a 'compulsion perhaps stronger than any — though unrecognised' (30). Again, Kate O'Brien paints an ambiguous family portrait. Lorna Reynolds' assertion about the Considines holds equally true for the Mulqueens: 'While the family nurtures, it also constricts its members' (43).

In her first two novels Kate O'Brien introduces what will remain one of her most persistent and passionate themes: the costs as well as the rewards of ardent familial attachments. Lorna Reynolds indicates that Kate O'Brien writes empirically: 'Sensibility — indeed, hyper-sensitiveness — to family feeling remained strongly implanted in Kate O'Brien all her life... Long removed from Ireland, intellectually independent, out of sympathy with a great deal that had developed in the country during her absence', she was still 'emotionally involved with her family... anxious not to upset or disturb her sisters... determined, especially, to do them all credit in Limerick' (30-31).

The Forsyte Saga may have been Kate O'Brien's model for establishing the public position of her characters and examining the power of the family within a social context, but its perspective was too panoramic for the study of an intense, solitary struggle. For this, Kate O'Brien found her model among novels in which the central character's actions reflect the authority of the familiar in moral choice. In several of her essays, Kate O'Brien suggests the particular influence of George Eliot's *The Mill on the Floss* on her development as a novelist. It is, for example, the only novel she mentions by name in *Presentation Parlour* as having given her special pleasure in her teens. Her 'unkind and mean', but literary, Auntie Mick had lent her the book and took great delight in her appreciation:

'So you are liking *The Mill on the Floss?*... If you're interested in [it] I'll tell you about George Eliot.' And she did. She told me what she knew, and it was accurate, about the childhood, youth and young womanhood of Mary Ann Evans, and roused in me much of what was her own passionate feeling for that young and formidable bluestocking. Spread over readings, she told me of the great novels I would read later, of the worldly success and the mastery. (102)

In 'George Eliot: A Moralising Fabulist', a paper presented before the Royal Society of Literature in 1951, seventeen years after she wrote *The*

Ante-Room, Kate O'Brien referred to *The Mill on the Floss* as one of those works that 'seemed to stamp themselves, all shining upon one's vision, never to be dimmed . . . never to be less than miracles'.[2] And, although she found it 'uneven' (41), and the 'weakest at its very centre' (40) among George Eliot's novels, she nevertheless insisted that in it, Eliot moved 'the English novel miles ahead of itself', propelling its 'whole moral conception' forward so that as a form, the novel could become the instrument of 'an active and unblinking conscience' (40). *The Mill on the Floss* haunted the adult Kate O'Brien as well as the teenager. It remained 'a book of great nostalgic power' (41).

In her essay, which attempts a brief assessment of George Eliot's 'best excellences' (45), Kate O'Brien concentrates on the writer's skill as a moralist. Examining George Eliot, she also suggests her own similar literary goals:

> she was always primarily concerned for the moral development of her characters whilst being able to expose their dilemmas with the purest possible detachment, yet tenderly. The right and wrong of each heart — its *own* right and wrong — was her quarry; and she would spare no trouble to catch up with it, and study it calmly in relation to its place and nature. (45)

Even to the most foolish of her characters, George Eliot adds 'the torture, the dignity of conscience — of scruple', the awareness of their own 'moral responsibility'. Her casts are thus devoid of 'lovely innocents' and 'dashing, careless boys'. It is their acute sense of accountability that makes all of George Eliot's characters 'touching' and worthy of our emotional investment. They are never 'pitiful victim[s]' but 'struggler[s] in the spirit' who 'confront' their destinies (40).

Kate O'Brien identified strongly with the morality of George Eliot's novels. She once said, 'I am a moralist, in that I see no story unless there is a moral conflict, and the old-fashioned sense of the soul and its troubling effect in human affairs.'[3] Nearly all her characters possess some degree of moral sensitivity.

As Vivian Mercier has argued, 'in her novels there are virtually no unsympathetic characters; she attempts to understand and sympathize with *everybody* . . . With her, to understand is to forgive'.[4] Kate O'Brien is not prey to moral absolutes; she insists that each ethical choice has its context, that the 'right and wrong of each heart' grows 'in relation to its place and nature' (45). Like Eliot, she wishes to penetrate the 'quarry', to ferret out the particular significance of a moral decision within an individual psyche.

Moreover, *The Mill on the Floss* showed Kate O'Brien the shape duty takes when early experience is the individual's greatest authority. Maggie Tulliver's choices were determined by her childhood. She acted according not to what would come, but to what had been, and although her past was far from ideal, its power over her emotions was greater than any other. George Eliot's 'shining' work had just this sort of effect on Kate O'Brien's developing literary vision.

Not only are there general parallels in moral perspective between *The Mill on the Floss* and *The Ante-Room,* but specific resemblances in plot and characterisation point to the pervasive influence of George Eliot's novel. Agnes's renunciation of her love for Vincent O'Regan is reminiscent both of Maggie Tulliver's friendship with Philip Wakem and of her relationship with Stephen Guest, her cousin Lucy's all-but-affianced suitor. In each of Maggie's liaisons, familial feeling determines her choices and forms the framework of her morality, regardless of personal desire. The past proves stronger than Maggie's love, first for Philip, later for Stephen. 'I desire no future', she says, 'that will break the ties of the past . . . the tie to my brother is one of the strongest. I can do nothing willingly that will divide me always from him'.[5] Maggie's drowning, locked in Tom's arms, must have seemed to Kate O'Brien the very paradigm of the primacy of kinship.

Similarly, in *The Ante-Room* Kate O'Brien insists that the first human duty is to affirm the claims of childhood. It is ironic, but consistent with the theme of *The Ante-Room,* that, by falling in love with Vincent, Agnes secures permanently her ties to her sister and the rest of her family. The imagined relationship violates every precept, but her passion for Vincent is so intense that it is unlikely that Agnes will ever love again. Her sister, like Maggie's brother, will remain her paramount attachment throughout her life.

If *The Ante-Room* is deeply influenced by George Eliot's novel, it remains tied to its 'place and nature'; it is a bourgeois, Irish Catholic version of *The Mill on the Floss.* Agnes Mulqueen acknowledges, attempts to suppress, and then renounces her love for her brother-in-law on grounds that, if reminiscent of Maggie Tulliver's rejection of Stephen Guest, also grow directly from the idiosyncrasies of her background. She enjoys all the extravagances arrayed in *Without My Cloak* and is governed by the same concern for appearances, family loyalty, and religious ritual. Internalising the repression endemic to Mellick, Agnes accedes to the 'Christian and social duty' that combined with 'sisterly love to make one foolish craving of hers impossible'. Her 'brains and blood and training found them justified and her desire insane. It followed it must die'.[91] (240)

Catholicism in *The Ante-Room* is both an internal article of belief and a social reality, a psychological as well as a communal catalyst. It is the centre of the novel and the centre of Agnes's character and, even more than her wealth or bourgeois social status, it separates her from

Maggie Tulliver. The time and place Kate O'Brien has chosen emphasise the religiosity of *The Ante-Room*. The action is contained solely within and about Roseholm, where Agnes's mother, Teresa, lies dying of cancer, and in the nearby Jesuit church where Agnes confesses. It is set on three consecutive holy days in the Catholic calendar: the Eve of All Saints, the Feast of All Saints, and the Feast of All Souls. The family has dedicated these days to prayer for Teresa, whose devotion to Reggie, her dissolute son (modelled most probably on Kate O'Brien's only maternal uncle)[6] sustains her as she awaits a sign that God will fill the vacuum in Reggie's life that her death will create.

Agnes's faith functions both regressively and repressively, yet Kate O'Brien, a 'Catholic agnostic' since her school days ,[7] neither fails to appreciate nor satirises the piety that infuses the Mulqueen home and shapes the activities of its tragic days. Rather, although painfully sensitive to the negative effects of Irish Catholicism upon her as a woman and a writer, she treats it with the utmost credibility and respect. In the midst of the Triduum, on the morning of the Feast of All Saints — and set at the very mid-point of the novel — Father Tom, Teresa's brother, offers Mass in the dressing room that adjoins Teresa's bedroom, the ante-room of the title. Reverence envelops the supreme moment of the service. Kate O'Brien captures the holiness of the rite with a depth of human feeling and spiritual bonding that transcends individual experience:

deeply stilled in their spirits by the quiet, well-known prayers and movements of the priest, they were able when he cried out: 'Sursum Corda', to answer voicelessly . . . 'Habemus ad Dominum'. Thus through a brief din of 'Holy, Holy, Holy!' they reached the quietest moment of their faith, a moment so still that bells must ring and sometimes guns must sound to make it humanly bearable. (173)

Benevolently, the author demonstrates the power and appeal of her characters' faith. It binds 'this assemblage of isolated hearts' (173) to each other as well as to 'some unknown, external will'. Their fervent Catholicism does not appear, as it occasionally did in *Without My Cloak,* as social convention; rather, it is an undeniable reality that imparts structure and meaning to their lives, never more exquisitely than at the moment of consecration:

It was the hour in which these souls understood that the easy sounding phrase 'God's will', was not a mere cloud with which to soften inconsistencies, but the name of an aged principle out of which a million million patterns and formulas could rise, but which spans and covers all. The hour when the most stupid felt, rather than saw, the point of view of God. (175)

All the participants accept the miracle of the Mass. The force of their faith is replicated in the transformations of the author's language. As the simple phrase 'God's Will' becomes a 'million million patterns', an 'aged principle', that 'covers all', so the ritual becomes, in the reader's eye, a convening of souls far greater in number than the gathered human family, far greater in time than the earthly moments for which it lasts. What might appear mere verbal convention becomes supernatural truth.

Agnes's faith is as affecting within her as it is around her; it frames her thoughts, directs her actions, and keeps her safe for Mellick. Kate O'Brien suggests the centrality of religion in Agnes's consciousness early in the narrative when, as the mass bells herald the start of the day, Agnes thinks about her mother's illness and her sister's unhappy marriage. Her thoughts lead her to prayer, which for her is no perfunctory ritual, but a serious meditation on a paradox she sees in prayer itself: 'Prayer that should humble [gives] relief by self-inflation'. She wonders how to 'accept and honour God and yet steer clear of heroics. Would it be more honest, more prayerful, not to pray at all? But that would be a deliberate spiritual pride, and would lead her further into the desert than she had courage to go' (10).

Agnes has none of the romanticism that occasionally crept into Caroline's religious practices in *Without My Cloak*. Her thoughtful, intense consciousness puts its faith to the test, examines every thought and every impulse scrupulously. She cannot corrupt her religious obligations with hypocrisy. Agnes, whose habit it had been to confess once each week and receive Communion twice, has not done so for nearly three months — not since Vincent and Marie-Rose's last visit. To 'her strong and honest faith this state of things was very startling'. And yet, because she is so honest, so meticulous in her self-observation, Agnes can correct her moral failure, can give up her thoughts of Vincent, only if she truly wishes to. She neglects for a time 'a growing sense of guilt against her mother, for whose health and peace the rest of the family were now leaving no effort untried of prayer and self-denial' (34). Even the strength of conscience that marks all of Kate O'Brien's heroines cannot yet return Agnes to the full observance of her faith. Father Tom sweeps her back, however, when he calls for a Triduum of prayer for Teresa, which Marie-Rose and Vincent will attend. There is nothing automatic or superficial about Agnes's faith. After profound soul-searching, faced with confronting the pair uncleansed of her illicit feelings, Agnes renews her moral obligation.

At every turn, Kate O'Brien shows that Agnes's bonds to her faith and to her family are not simply intense, they are inseparable. The thought of one leads her to thought of the other. Kate O'Brien describes, for example, how Agnes looks at the priest, her uncle, 'with gentleness . . .

His faith, more florid than her own, though not more natural, had power to move her, and constantly he touched her deeply by the tender unceasing fret he carried in his heart for his dying sister' (46). Tom's example moves Agnes to confess, to overcome her passion, to let go of Vincent:

God must be stormed. He was omnipotent and omniscient, but He had arranged human things so that they should work upwards only by guess and faith, by intuitions almost entirely blind . . . No use in folding hands before the problem of God's Will and His incomprehensible attitude to suffering . . . If prayer came naturally — and nothing was more natural to Agnes — now was its special time . . . pray, if that seemed the true thing to do. Pray, and forget or forsake those little petty secrets of the selfish heart that made prayer difficult. (50)

As Agnes submits to training, so ingrained that it is 'at least half herself' (82-3), we experience the catharsis with her, but we will also feel the momentary inadequacy of her confession when she later is overwhelmed by her passion for Vincent. For the moment, however, faith and morality triumph as Agnes resumes her Christian duty and filial obligation and can greet Marie-Rose and Vincent unburdened:

how delicious to have this sister here again! And now, with heart cleansed of offence against her, now cooled by the antiseptic of confession, to be able to turn to her, with the old, deep, unstained affection — it was glorious! To have been able, after ten weeks of miserable dreaming and self-pity, to enter a room where he was and look at him and feel no fear or heart or tenderness — oh God, that was bliss, that was a miracle! (106)

But if, as the priest has instructed Agnes in confession, earthly love is mortal, it dies not without a struggle. Agnes's ultimate test is Vincent himself. His expression of love for her destroys her self-confidence and her sense of security; the naturalness of his touch moves her more than she had thought possible: 'Her nature was as if hypnotised by a revelation of its own weakness, even when tested in an hour of special strength. But how could she have known that his hand had such a power in it?' (139).

Vincent's hand on her shoulder, Agnes hears the 'little cough' of Sister Emmanuel, her mother's night attendant. In that sound, 'almost holy in its repression', Kate O'Brien makes clear how seamlessly the Church has moulded Agnes's inner life and tied her to her family. The nun's stifled breath reminds Agnes of 'the idea of holiness, the idea of pain. It brought back prayer and duty and the memory of her own confession'. It drives Agnes's spirit from its 'moment of rightness under [Vincent's] loved hand, to its outer, older knowledge of another rectitude'. As Sister

Emmanuel coughs once more, Agnes returns to herself, to her faith, and to her family. 'Never again', she hears herself saying. Leaving Vincent, she knocks at her mother's door, repeating: 'Oh, Mother of the Word Incarnate, despise not my petitions —' (140).

It is the nun's quiet cough, a simple sound rather than an extended theological argument, that is Kate O'Brien's most dramatic symbol of the intimate, personal meaning of religion in this domestic setting. It confirms Agnes's internal mandates: repression of personal desire and concern for her family. The nun calls Agnes to her duty as social and familial pressures called to Caroline and Denis. The author suggests that Agnes may still waver, but she will withstand Vincent's persistence and his seemingly fantastic offer that they go together into exile. Rejecting a course that Kate O'Brien's later heroines will accept, Agnes insists that Vincent believes as she does, 'that in the end the Church is right' (251). It is the Church, where their convictions inevitably unite, that keeps Agnes and Vincent apart.

But Kate O'Brien insists that what most moves Agnes to reject Vincent is her regard for Marie-Rose, the bond from childhood that, like Maggie Tulliver's feeling for Tom, sustained and nurtured her, helped form a strong self-image. The standards of Agnes's morality lie not in rules or rituals dedicated to an abstract deity, but in the conduct of human relationships. Agnes dismisses Vincent, not simply because his wife is her sister, but because his wife is Marie-Rose, to whom she has 'related everything in life' (265), and whose greatest kindness remains the source of Agnes's persistent loyalty: 'Once someone told me I was the plainest girl in the school, and Marie-Rose gave me no peace until I told her what had upset me. The revenge she took! The way she lampooned that plain little girl before the Junior School! I think I'd have died for her that night!' (265). Furthermore, Agnes knows that she is the 'only living soul [Marie-Rose] feels safe with' (264). Thus, no matter how much she loves Vincent, she cannot destroy that older, greater unity. Agnes is a prisoner of her first feelings. Even if Vincent should physically possess her, awakening her sexual desire, Agnes's past would still hold strong. Kate O'Brien explains that 'violence and passion would have their tortured minute if he insisted, but they could not retrace, unplait, unravel the long slow weaving of childhood' (267-8).

But even this characterisation of intense familial love has its share of ambivalence. More delicately and less ironically than in *Without My Cloak*, Kate O'Brien suggests that the love that binds her characters to each other has its destructive aspects. As in her later novel, *The Flower of May*, sisterly love becomes a regressive force. Agnes and Marie-Rose so insulate each other that neither need ever grow up; their affection precludes for Agnes a fulfilling, complete life as a wife and mother.

Teresa's martyrdom for her ruined, syphilitic son so consumes her that she withdraws from the rest of her family. Her maternal devotion has driven Reggie into an infantilised dependency; he denies both his illness and its restrictions. Speaking from deep within her characters, Kate O'Brien evinces the sympathy for them and their viewpoints that she ascribes to George Eliot, even as she indicates that their love for each other deludes and damages them.

Although Kate O'Brien turns inward in this novel, her characters move within a larger context. Those on the periphery of the Mulqueen circle — an elegant English nobleman-doctor, an impoverished nurse, and an Irish country doctor — suggest that more than the emotional life at Roseholm is eroding. The bemused cancer specialist Sir Godfrey Bartlett-Crowe reminds the reader of the social and political fires that redden beyond Roseholm's gates. To Sir Godfrey it first seems 'absurd . . . to plunge right into the murderous and stormy south, to stay in the home of a real Irishman, and waste twenty-four hours, and perhaps encounter danger in so doing'. But 'the carriage and pair' that meet him outside Mellick station reassure him. 'The spaciousness and warmth of Roseholm' is a surprise. Sir Godfrey's host, Danny Mulqueen, may be 'vulgar-looking' but he is also 'amusingly mild'. Only Reggie displeases Sir Godfrey, but the doctor shrugs off that unsavoury impression 'in the comfort of his bedroom, where a great fire, a mighty bed and the hospitable and deferential fussings in and out with hot water of a venerable housemaid . . . most consolingly [adjust] his notions of native Irish life' (202-5).

Kate O'Brien's allusions belie Sir Godfrey's pleasant illusion, however. Her narrative subtly informs the reader that the Ireland of Roseholm belongs only to a very few and will soon escape even them. The evictions, the Land League, Michael Davitt, the boycott, to which Sir Godfrey briefly refers, are excluded as pointedly from *The Ante-Room* as from the lives it depicts. Its characters mention the land agitation raging in the countryside in just one conversation; Parnell, then at the height of his powers, they mention twice, each time, in frivolous and superficial chat, 'politics-and-state-of-the-country talk . . . full of wise saws' (212).

The outside world, however, is fast encroaching. It has already invaded Roseholm in the figure of Nurse Cunningham, whose mundane position and personal catechism contrast markedly with the Mulqueens'. 'Comfort [is] not an impossible thing for a sensible woman to achieve' (147), Nurse Cunningham insists. Above all, Nurse Cunningham is a sensible woman. Hard-working since her seventeenth year, she is nevertheless financially insecure. If, by marrying Reggie and caring for him, she can live the life she observes at Roseholm, she will happily forego such luxuries as love and passion.

Solitary and unconnected, 'energetic and level-headed' (37), Nurse Cunningham is the future. Her life, less violent than the one to which Sir Godfrey alludes, and less degrading than Christina's in *Without My Cloak,* suggests what awaits the woman who has no family to protect her or has one but chooses to free herself from its refuge. In today's terms a professional woman, she is the antithesis of Agnes and Marie-Rose. From the start of the story, when she tells Teresa the day and the date without knowing the Saint's Day, Nurse Cunningham makes it clear that her past denied sanctimony as well as grandeur. Nurse Cunningham pits pragmatism against piety. With no thought that God will provide, she cleverly arranges her marriage with Reggie, acquiring at last the social and economic status that Agnes and Marie-Rose have always taken for granted.

The conclusion of *The Ante-Room* reiterates its conflicting world views. On the one hand there is Teresa, whose religious passion has been directed at her son's salvation, and who sees his marriage as God's will, the answer to her prayers:

This woman who in middle life had seen her greatest treasure, the apple of her eye, destroy himself, and who had had to live watching the slow extension of that ruin, this woman who had borne the fluctuating tortures of three years of cancer, and now had about two months of pain and unreality to look to — at her eleventh hour, with no powers left her but those of faith and sentiment, was purely happy, entirely and childishly grateful to God, without pang or afterthought — because her ruined son would have a custodian when she was gone. God had heard her one prayer, her miserable, human and weak intercession . . . 'Oh, but He was mighty and infinite of heart, the ever-merciful and omnipotent God, the King of Kings, the Son of Mary . . . Oh, Reggie, Reggie — God is good . . . (288)

On the other hand there is Nurse Cunningham's business-like, almost mercantile, reaction that immediately follows Teresa's paean: 'listening, looking, and considerably moved by the happiness which her decision had brought, [Nurse Cunningham] assured herself that she was giving good measure in return for what she might get. The bargain would be fair' (289). Nurse Cunningham's insinuation of herself into the family contrasts with Teresa's belief that Reggie's marriage is part of God's design. As she takes over Teresa's place in Reggie's life, Nurse Cunningham represents inevitable, impending change. She is an outsider, but more successful than Richard Froude in *The Ante-Room* or Angèle Maury in *The Last of Summer* at finding a place for herself within her new milieu. Hers may be a Pyrrhic victory, but she has opened the doors of Roseholm; she has gained access to the bourgeoisie.

A disturbing figure to Agnes and Marie-Rose, Nurse Cunningham evokes little charity from them. They judge her actions harshly because they cannot comprehend a life deprived of their daily comforts. A precursor of the 'Misses' of Altorno in *Mary Lavelle,* Nurse Cunningham may hint at the circumstances the author feared after her father died; still a young woman then, Kate O'Brien could no longer count on the comforts of her Limerick home.[8] Because her religion is opportunism, clearheadedness and compromise, Nurse Cunningham is what Agnes and Marie-Rose will never be — and what Kate O'Brien may have feared she might have to become.

Dr Curran bridges the gap between the piety of the Mulqueens and the pragmatism of Nurse Cunningham. Joan Ryan has pointed out that 'everyone' in *The Ante-Room* is 'unmistakably devoutly Catholic . . . [The] interior life of the characters', and particularly the inner life of Agnes, is 'dictated in its every breath by the dictates of Catholicism and especially by the hellfire and brimstone ultimatum preached with rising and crashing fist from the Redemptorist pulpit in Limerick'.[9] Joan Ryan, however, fails to recognise the variety of religious experience that Kate O'Brien unveils in this novel. Showing the workings of belief within an individual consciousness — 'God's Will' has a 'million million patterns' — Kate O'Brien is ruthlessly honest and realistic. Each character's faith differs from every other's. Dr Curran's is as different from Teresa's and Agnes's as theirs is from Nurse Cunningham's. He is a 'rationalist in the idiom of his mind, Catholic in tradition and practice, a man eager to harness feeling into usefulness' (57). Dr Curran does not turn to prayer to fulfil his deepest wish; he views his religion as a reasonable way for human beings to organise their emotions, to regulate their lives. He has little need of Church or prayer beyond the usual observances. He takes

prayer as a matter of course, a natural human impulse which it was not his business, or perhaps anyone's, to explain. As a doctor he observed it to be the most salutary of medicines. The pros and cons of religion never stayed his thought, life as he found it being the field of his concern. And in that field it seemed to him that the Catholic Church provided as good a system as might be found for keeping the human animal in order — a necessity which he emphatically accepted. A good system because, through thick and thin, it exacted a soul of every man and instilled in the very lowest of its creatures an innocent familiarity with the things not apprehended of the flesh. Mysticism and its chance to ennoble, or at least to alleviate, granted, Doctor Curran would be rationalistic, as indeed he observed the Church to be, in his manipulation and acceptance of the religious impulse. (67)

Kate O'Brien sympathises with and accepts the religious perspectives of all her characters, but Agnes suggests most conspicuously that older form of faith that Kate O'Brien once held and apparently left behind. Nurse Cunningham points to an atheistic future. But in offsetting Agnes's faith and the nurse's practicality, Dr Curran seems to speak as personally as any of her characters for the mature Kate O'Brien, suggesting her view towards her 'hereditary' (67) Catholicism. In his religious attitudes, Dr Curran, like Nurse Cunningham, underscores the parochialism within Roseholm, even as he would choose to become a part of the household. His rationalism, too, compels the reader to question whether orthodoxy functions for the Mulqueens like Teresa's morphia delusions, blocking out the truth that they wish not to see. Is the whole family, so filled with the certainty of its faith, equally deluded? Are all the Mulqueens dying, only dreaming a disfigured, diseased reality, momentarily disguised?

The suggestion that the family may not be as stable an institution as it appears pervades *Without My Cloak* and undercuts its conclusion. It also concludes *The Ante-Room*. Vincent's fantasy, as he pulls the trigger of his suicide gun, glows, not with visions of Agnes, his mature love, but with every detail of his dead mother's smile; and, like the aura surrounding Anna Hennessy, that golden sunlight seems eclipsed in clouds. Although his death preserves Agnes for her family, Vincent's suicide is a weak ending to this powerful book. The final words should be Agnes's. She has made the righteous decision; everything she has known or been taught has led to it. And yet we see her choice of Marie-Rose above all else as we see her mother's love for Reggie and Vincent's passion for his dead mother: as a retreat from the future. As Maggie's death in *The Mill on the Floss* implies, so does Vincent's suicide in *The Ante-Room* suggest: a life predicated in the past is doomed.

Four

Mary Lavelle

Mary Lavelle[1] marks a turning-point in Kate O'Brien's fictional journey. Not only is this the first of her novels to take place outside Ireland, but it also presents a protagonist who consciously violates the tenets in which her previous characters so assiduously believed. Written in 1936, on the eve of the Spanish Civil War, *Mary Lavelle* is more than a commentary on the conflicts between family and freedom, duty and defiance, and domestic and foreign influences. It is also Kate O'Brien's elegy for an alternative to Ireland's claustrophobic society.

In contrasting *Mary Lavelle* with *A Portrait of the Artist as a Young Man,* Katie Donovan mistakenly asserts that whereas Joyce's novel 'concentrates on . . . the shedding of old ties until [Stephen Dedalus] is alone and rootless', Kate O'Brien's insists on Mary's 'return to the familiar structures which dominate her close-knit community'.[2] But Kate O'Brien avers explicitly that, though Mary's self-assessments are governed by lessons learned in Mellick, her actions will remove her from that community. As the author's first fictional venture away from Mellick and its mores, *Mary Lavelle* implies the direction of her later works.

Kate O'Brien's reverence for Spanish individualism provides the thematic framework for *Mary Lavelle*. The novel's central characters face private dilemmas that echo the larger social issues confronting modern Spain; their tenuous autonomy mirrors Spain's threatened freedom. Tracing Mary's self-discovery, from the exposure of her passionate individuality to her painful submission to old social and moral codes, Kate O'Brien suggests Spain's imminent fate. Mary's return to Ireland and inevitable rejection at the hands of conventional morality are — like the death of the patriarch Don Pablo Areavaga, the novel's most powerful emblem of Spanish individualism — the fictional equivalent of the Fascistic 'day of uniformity'[3] awaiting Spain.

Although seemingly a personal story, *Mary Lavelle* is Kate O'Brien's most political work thus far. In *Without My Cloak* and *The Ante-Room* the characters ignored the social upheaval raging about them, their disassociation a symptom of their distance from the mainstream of Irish life and a symbol of their affluence. In *Mary Lavelle* the characters are politically active, and their activity reflects the personal struggles which provide the novel's central themes. If *Mary Lavelle,* the novel, defines more explicitly than Kate O'Brien's earlier works the shortcomings of middle-class Irish Catholic life, Mary Lavelle, the individual, in her quest for independence, personifies the author's dissatisfaction with that life. In *Mary Lavelle,* characters from a social class as privileged as that in *Without My Cloak* and *The Ante-Room* shed their mantles of social withdrawal and work to relieve the pain of common families. Don Pablo and Juanito, Areavaga father and son, express their singularity by addressing the problems of the less fortunate. Their proletarian sympathies and political preferences, Don Pablo's anarchism and Juanito's Communism, distinguish them from their peers.

Kate O'Brien's third novel is, to a degree, a fictionalisation of her experiences abroad in 1922-23. Mary Lavelle and Kate O'Brien both left comfort and security in Ireland to spend a year as a Miss in Spain. Each awakened to, and suffered for, her passion — personal in one case, nationalistic in the other. The prologue to *Mary Lavelle* wittily describes the trunk of a 'Miss' crossing the Pyrenees. It suggests that Mary's passage from the innocence of Mellick to the sexual passion of Cabantes will be a long journey into the self. Her trunk contains, 'like those persons in its place of origin who packed and labelled it, the air of never having wandered far from parish bounds' (xix). As the Spanish customs official delves into its bowels, examining its unprepossessing belongings and uncovering the Miss's 'equipment for the decent life', its owner 'grows fidgety' (xx). The innards of Mary's trunk — her private self — have yet to acquire distinguishing traits; they have been 'packed' and 'labelled' by others at home. The searching, disruptive hands of the customs official augur both the bestirring of Mary's sheltered vision and her discovery 'that what each man calls his own reality advances on him and shapes itself as much from without as from within, from accident as from preconception' (xxi). Having known only the changeless patterns of Mellick, Mary cannot guess how life in Spain will change her.

The ironic tone as the novel opens foreshadows the psychological drama to come. Setting out with a confidence that the reader recognises as naïvité, Mary asserts as universal and eternal the values that have governed her earlier life. Her convictions, so firmly rooted in her Irish past, weaken as the ethos of Spanish life intrudes on her awareness. At the novel's end, when Mary's Spanish education is complete, neither innocence nor dramatic irony remains.

In *The Ante-Room* Kate O'Brien established the Mass as the novel's spiritual and literal centre, signifying the characters' sense of duty and the order and emotional truths that governed their lives. In *Mary Lavelle,*

Kate O'Brien uses the bullfight to represent the same elements and to unite the political and personal dimensions of the novel. The *corrida* defines both Juanito Areavaga's politics, a reflection of Kate O'Brien's own, and Mary's quest for self-fulfilment and self-expression. A Republican, communistically inspired, but committed to the uniqueness of the individual, Juanito sees the bullfight as the glorification of that uniqueness. Interpreting the bullfight's social implications, he insists that although Communism may meet men's basic needs, it can never destroy the Spanish reverence for the individual, that after Communism has come and gone in Spain, the people will have both their bread and bulls: 'Bread for everyone as soon as possible, bread for belly and heart and brain — but in the end . . . not bread alone. *Pan y toros!*'(161).

If Juanito recognises the bullfight's political significance, Mary responds to it as a revelation of the paradoxes from which her Irish existence has shielded her. Described as 'death and horror presented theatrically and really, both at once . . . as symbolical and suggestive and heartrending as the greatest poetry, and . . . as brutal and shameless as the lowest 'human impulse' (140), the bullfight teaches Mary that passion and beauty can both charm and maim. It is at the *corrida* that Mary first witnesses, in one moment, the contradictions of human life and the power of each person to determine his destiny. The bullfight expresses all the individualism that life in Mellick denies.

Mary has been in Spain only six weeks when she attends the bullfight. At home in Ireland, she and her fiancé John MacCurtain had agreed that she should not 'distress herself by seeing one'. 'Tender-hearted' to the point of absurdity about 'all helpless and dependent things', she would, they predicted, 'loathe it' (106). But as her affection for Spain grows, so does her ability to speak its language and read its newspapers — a most unusual accomplishment among Misses. The daily accounts of 'wounds, deaths, and victories; disgrace and glory; music, ovations, the round of the ring; the ear and the tail' (107) pique her curiosity. Mary attends a bullfight seeking an explanation for the apparant inconsistencies that permit so friendly and easy-going a people to enjoy 'the butchery of bulls and horses' (108).

She better understands the Spanish character when she experiences the paradoxical emotions of the *corrida* and responds with an exhilaration equal to any Spaniard's. In awe of the bullfight's beauty and its contrasting 'news of life's possible pain' (116), Mary does not yet perceive what the reader certainly knows — how much her few hours in the bullring have changed her. At this point, she recognises only 'the difference between shock and revulsion'; young, virginal, and virtuous, she has learnt 'that emotion at its most crude can by relation to a little art enchant, overwhelm and seem eternal' (129).

In language rife with sexual overtones, Kate O'Brien reveals that the bullfight is Mary's preparation for Juanito and for all that Spain will teach her: the 'wound of the bullfight' is 'the gateway through which Spain had entered in and taken her' (128). Although Mary believes that she is in love with John, she has never felt passion for him; his kisses even repel her. Her Spanish 'John', on the other hand, arouses both a passion and a pain that Mary has never known. Indeed, after her long journey to the bullfight — a psychological distance as great as Ireland's geographic removal from Spain — Mary refuses to read a letter from John that awaits her. She cannot return to the staid numbness of her Irish life.

Mellick, where Mary claims to have 'left her heart' — if not her passion — becomes 'remote and cloudy . . . out of focus' (20) as she experiences the immediacies of life in Cabantes. Under the florid Spanish sky, surrounded by glittering water, gardenias, and camellias in colourful pots, Mary remembers only a fog-blanketed Ireland, a childhood and youth of unquestioned sameness. The fog had engulfed Mary, together with her environment, her family, and John, even as it had engulfed the land. Spain assaults her sense of herself, in which, like her trunk, everything has it place. Reluctantly, she acknowledges the restlessness this country has induced:

She supposed she was homesick, so unaccountably heavy was her heart. She felt alien, dejected, out of tune. Almost as if she had been injured by this innocent place as if it sought to wound her. She thought of Mellick and of how lovely it would be to hear voices that she understood. (142)

As Mary recalls Mellick, images of a mournful stagnation flood her mind. Nevertheless, she tries to convince herself that her personal truth remains

where her own speech rang and her heart had formed its unpretentious habits. She had no Spaniard's need of a brutal and realistic manipulation of symbols; there was philosophic instruction and to spare in routine and decorum, in the simple and restrained ways of happiness and faith which she and John together understood . . . Her natural place was . . . in the rainy street of childhood where every sound and change of light was as natural as sleeping and waking, where she was known and where true love waited for her, where she had given her pledge of lifelong love. (142)

But Kate O'Brien shows us that the the seeds of Mary's personal and social rebellion were already planted in Mellick. Her father, who comes from 'indolent "squireen" stock', is an unhappy, disaffected country doctor, devoid of 'either sexual or intellectual vitality' (23-4). A widower, whose six children cause him only anguish and dismay, he chooses paths for them that reflect his conservative background. In 1917, he fervently hopes to dispose of his eldest son by procuring a commission for him in the Munster Fusiliers, but Jimmy, 'finding the fight for his individuality severe' (27), instead joins the IRA, spends time in jail, and stages a hunger strike. Mary cycles to villages and farms near Mellick on dangerous errands for him and his flying column. Anticipating her father's response to the consequences 'were his house searched by Auxiliaries and his eldest daughter put in jail' (25), she suggests that her actions have as much to do with protesting against Dr Lavelle's values as they have with politics. But with the truce of 1920, the radical activities of brother and sister alike subside, and, in a vain search for freedom, Jimmy leaves for Dublin and then America. Their younger brother Donal escapes a job in the Bank of Ireland by finding a position 'of the most miserable kind on a Dublin newspaper' (26) and then a slightly less miserable one in Leeds. But to Mary, Donal's freedom looks like happiness.

Without her brothers, Mary feels empty in Mellick; her father refuses to finance training for her employment and withholds the inheritance left by her grandmother. Mary fills her time with household duties and waits. In the winter of 1919, consumed with thoughts of Jim's marching to arms, Mary meets John MacCurtain, a recently demobilised major in the Fusiliers, who joined with the British to help 'gallant little Belgium'. He is kind, decent, and the personification of those values that Jim and Donal had struggled to flee. When he falls in love with Mary, John's mission becomes simply to build a satisfying life for the two of them in Mellick.

In the character of John, Kate O'Brien paints an ambivalent portrait of both the complacency and decency of most Mellick men. He is content never to examine the code by which he lives or to ask himself how it has become his directive. At home, Mary had recognised this foible in her fiancé and the limitations it imposed on their communication. She accepted it, however, for John's goodness, his aestheticism, 'his power to weave dreams of a dignified and fruitful married life' (136) compensated for his constricted awareness of what lay outside his limited view. To Mary, John represents Ireland, and since leaving both, she has been troubled. John

had sometimes in his letters tramped over her news and views with a heavier authority than she found patience for. Now and then she had had to put a letter aside half-read and wheedle herself into good-humoured affection for the writer before she could continue it . . . It did not occur to her that all these things of Spain that she chronicled for him and he dismissed impatiently were only unnecessary barriers between them in his eyes, whereas they were a part of everyday life to her now and by that insidiously endeared. (138-9)

As Mary becomes increasingly offended by John's disquieting traits and considers their portent, we notice the differences between her and the characters in Kate O'Brien's earlier works. Although she retains an attachment to home and a reverence for the familiar very like those of Agnes Mulqueen and Caroline Lanigan, Mary has, in contrast, believed since childhood in an 'ever changing tissue of dreams', the notion of 'perpetual self government', in being 'a freelance always', belonging 'to no one place or family or person' (27). Agnes and Caroline could never have understood Mary's youthful wanderlust and adventurousness. Yet, describing her life with John in Mellick, Mary sounds very much like her fictional forebears, inextricably entangled in the webs of childhood. Mary and John are not drawn *to* each other, as she and Juanito are; they are joined *with* each other, almost involuntarily, by the shared continuity of their pasts; together they feel 'a great mingling of inherited sympathies and the tides of their peace . . . seem to overflow' (33). In Ireland, Mary's future is part of her past and her present. The 'tides of peace', however, recede in favour of a 'tiny hiatus between her life's two accepted phases' (34), those of being a daughter and becoming a wife. John's approval is essential, and she pleads for a year on her own. Winning the 'first real battle of her life' (35), Mary travels far from John, from all she is and from all she expects to be — to be a 'Miss' in Spain and to satisfy the 'dominant intention of childhood' (27) that she had fought to subdue.

The three young Areavaga daughters, Mary's charges, reflect the stages of individuation Mary will undergo. In a surprising chronological reversal that conveys Mary's self-discovery, it is the youngest, Milagros, who affects her most powerfully. In contrast to the eldest, the vain and frivolous Pilár, who embodies only the most superficial values of her class and social position, and the retiring middle daughter, the Anglophilic Nieves, Milagros is, like her father and brother, an intellectual. 'Cool beyond her years and though completely and traditionally religious', she examines, as Mary soon must, 'every phenomenon that [comes] her way, no matter how such might seem to threaten faith or morals' (129-30). Unique and so brilliant that her father jokes that perhaps she, rather than her brother, will fulfil his dream of having sired one of 'Spain's great men', Milagros is as drawn to Mary as Mary is to her. This fourteen-year-old philosopher is one of Kate O'Brien's most unrealistic characters, but her significance in the novel is clear, nevertheless. Silhouetting Mary against Milagros, a 'true Spaniard', Kate O'Brien reveals the extent of Mary's innocence.

Like her attraction to the bullfight, Mary's affection for Milagros functions in the novel as a symbol of the effect that Spain will have on her and as a measure of her alienation from her past. In his letters John reacts to Mary's accounts of Milagros:

'she sounds a nauseating little freak. Wants locking up in a reformatory, I'd say off-hand'. Mary had been annoyed by that. There's such a thing as being idiotically off-hand, Mr. Lawgiver, she had thought, laying down the letter. And the annoyance had induced a timid meditation on whether or not small recurrent clashes of points of view on external matters were of little or great import between two who proposed to marry. (136)

If Milagros represents Spanish wisdom and the lessons Mary will learn, the other Misses employed in Altorno suggest what Mary could become should she remain closed to the powerful stimuli around her. The others from 'that not easily definable section of society, the Irish Catholic middle-class' (92), transplanted to Spain yet untouched by the contact, convey unexpected, strong moral messages. They also poignantly portray the emptiness of lives lacking the comforts of home and family, foretelling what Mary will lose if she renounces John. Indeed, the Misses connote a paradox. Mary cannot imagine remaining isolated and removed from her adopted country as they have; on the other hand, to ignore them, to immerse herself in her new surroundings, to participate fully in Spanish life, is also to sever ties with all that has given her life meaning till now. Despite her differences from the Misses, Mary, by falling in love with Juanito, with the bullfight and with Spain, will become more like them: a modern woman who must work for her livelihood. Like Nurse Cunningham in *The Ante-Room,* she will struggle on her own. The irony here is that, in succumbing to Spain, Mary will grimly fulfill her childhood fantasy of endless wandering in the lonely rootlessness of the Miss Barkers and McMahons, or of the homosexual Agatha Conlon, tormented in her impossible love for Mary.

As Mary had earlier abandoned herself to the bullfight and to Spain, she now abandons her sexual innocence, and, peeling away her self-deception, she finally and freely gives herself to Juanito, fully aware of the implications. With the same naïveté with which she had earlier denied her seduction by Spain, Mary tries to disclaim her growing feelings for her employer's married son, indulging them while disavowing addiction. She tries to be prudent, reminding herself that Juanito is merely a new acquaintance — and married. As Agnes sought to dull her passion with religion, unable to mute her 'school girl malaise' (218), Mary seeks relief in recollections of Mellick, where

blessed mists and rain, and the old rules were absolute; there goodness held

its ground, and faith and promise were synonymous with love; there peace would
be rediscovered and knowledge of herself; there she would have her old bearings
and steer by them honestly and happily. Ah God, to be back there, back in her
own quiet heart, in coldness and tenderness . . . She had not known that life
and travel and experiment could maim one thus. (239-40)

But Mellick cannot shield Mary from Spain; old rules cannot protect
her from new feelings. Spain tears at the unity woven about her in
Ireland, the fabric of a community's values. The Spain in which Mary
settles withholds the moral absolutes to which she has been
accustomed; the ideas of sin and goodness may not mean what she
had been taught.

Like the bullfight, Juanito is a means to Mary's awakening. Since he
is married and, therefore, can pose no threat to her persistent need
for freedom, he becomes an ironic manifestation of her secret wish to
belong to no place and no person. His awkwardly placed appearance
late in the novel, after Mary has begun her self-discovery, suggests that
their love story is not as crucial to the novel as Mary's quest for
individuation and self-definition. Juanito is pivotal, however, as a
symbol of Mary's liberation from the 'terrifying peace' (142) and
permanent patterns of her childhood.

Not just Juanito but his entire family works changes in Mary. From
the moment Kate O'Brien introduces the Areavagas, their difference from
the Lavelles, as well as from the Considines and Mulqueens, is obvious.
Although as *haute bourgeois* and wealthy as their Irish counterparts in
the earlier novels, the Areavagas have been committed for generations
to social and economic fairness, declining bids to join the aristocracy.
Don Juan Areavaga, a very different patriarch from Honest John
Considine, began the family's tradition of public service. An opulent
man with a rich social conscience, he reviled 'the evil plight of the
industrial magnate' and painfully acknowledged that the 'circumstances
out of which his duties and privileges arose were founded on false
premises'. He strove to be a 'conscientious and enterprising employer'
and his 'experiments in the direction of social justice', particularly his
channelling of private profits for public purposes, 'were observed with
fear and discomfort by others of his caste'. He was 'Christian, cultured,
somewhat Jansenistic, [and] profoundly a Spaniard . . . convinced to the
last drop of his blood in the absolute dominion of personality over
system' (50).

Don Juan's eldest son, Pablo — a far cry, indeed, from the elitist,
politically indifferent Anthony Considine — inherited his father's
virtues, intellect, and individualism. More explosive than Don Juan, he
proposed to go further in industrial reform when he took control of
the family wealth and hoped to aid his ailing country by entering

political life. An idealist who cherished 'anarchist projects' for 'human justice and the betterment of his fellow men' (54), Don Pablo believed that drastic steps were necessary if Spain were to have an acceptable secular government in which liberty was available to every man. A man, he insisted, should have little sway over his neighbour. But Catholic as well as anarchist, Don Pablo held that religion was essential to human life, and, despite his loathing of institutions, he granted the Church a place in his political vision. Catholicism, even at its worst, appealed to him as 'the only system of faith at once impassioned and controlled', and he remained devoted to its ideals and many of its traditions. He gave shape to his unusual political creed through writing and oratory, applying 'his impossible theories against immediate issues' to arrive eventually perhaps at a 'practicable code and a movement' (61).

Kate O'Brien does not idealise the Areavagas, however, revealing that here too family constrains freedom and, in Don Pablo's case, precludes political action. His father and wife thwart him socially and intellectually. After years of bitterness, he accedes to their wishes. Retaining wealth enough for his family 'to live in suitable bourgeois state' (62), he divests himself of business and looks to his son Juanito for the fulfilment of his political hopes for Spain and for the emotional satisfaction he cannot find with his wife.

In this family history, Kate O'Brien shows us three generations of men in conflict with their ideals. As Don Pablo's dreams for Spain outstripped Don Juan's, so Juanito's radicalism surpasses Don Pablo's. Despite his devotion to the Catholic Church and his marriage to an aristocrat whose traditions embody the injustice and privilege he decries, Juanito is inspired by Communist ideology. He believes Communism, better than other political philosophies, prescribes the 'desperate remedies' needed to cure Spain's 'desperate diseases' (160). He strives to centralise Spain, create a slave-state, and see both later overthrown. Spanish individualism, the infallible respect for the unspoken mind of every fellow-man, would ensure that although Communism must come to Spain within fifty years, it would be gone within a hundred, 'leaving knowledge the only true good behind it' (161).

Juanito's political direction parallels Mary's personal course. Kate O'Brien suggests that these paths may converge in futility. Making clear the folly of the lovers' resistance to social and religious traditions, she implies that Juanito's utopian ideals may be as unattainable as his and Mary's passion. She insists that, for all its seeming reality, their love is merely illusion, forceful and enthralling, but illusion, nevertheless, because powerless to remove and replace the conventions that continue to govern their lives. As they express their feelings for the first time, Mary tells Juanito what she believes love to be:

'I've never been in love, Juanito — until now. So I used to think it a lovely, suitable thing, that would grow in its time. I thought I'd like the feeling and be able to manage it and make — people — happy through it. Just now I don't think it's like that.'

. . . 'It's not suitable or manageable. It blurs things, puts everything out of focus. It's not a thing to live with. It's a dream.'

. . . 'We'll never be given the chance to mix it with reality. Why, look where we have to come even to talk of it'

She jerked her head in indication of the rocks and golden hills. (247)

Even after the two have consummated their passion, Juanito asks Mary, 'Are you a fatal exception that makes splinters of everything normal? Or am I just vulgarly infatuated, and is this a showing up? Are you my true love — or an illusion?' They are both illusions, according to Mary, and 'there's nothing to be afraid of in that' (307).

Thus, although her defiance wanes, Mary is the first of Kate O'Brien's characters strong enough to crack the foundation that supports her identity. In the world of men and mores, however, old codes do not bend to romantic love; old codes are the rigid reality to which both Juanito and Mary must succumb. Their love is only an exquisite moment in lives that must be governed ultimately by older orders and older ways. They are hopeless victims, 'since, love as they might, their peace lay for each at last in his own breast, in his own nature, and in their natures framed in a million accidents of teaching, nationality and intention' (320-21). Dismissing Juanito's protests, Mary confronts the facts of their lives before they met:

If you were an American, say, and your wife had a little lost her interest in you, and divorce was part of the code and religion you were brought up in, and would not displace your ambition and ideals, and make you into a kind of exile without occupation — then you and I might have a clumsy sort of future to discuss. But as it is we haven't. We're Catholics, and you're a Spanish patriot and 'one of Spain's great men', and you have a wife and son to whom you are devoted, and your wife is devoted to you. So you see, our 'infatuation' is simply an uncomplicated pain which we must get over. (254)

Juanito works to salvage their romance even as Mary insists on the rules that she has known, resented, and flouted. She

lay under his hands and marvelled at her peace [thinking] of school and home, of John, of God's law and of sin, and did not let herself discard such thoughts. They existed, as real and true as ever, with all their traditional claims on her — but this one claim was his, and she would answer it, taking the consequences. (308)

Mary knows that her passion for Juanito will destroy her life with John. She will have to leave Mellick and become the rootless wanderer about whom she had once so happily fantasised. With the vision of the Misses of Altorno haunting her, she heads homeward to face John with her defenceless story. 'And afterwards — she would take her god-mother's hundred pounds and go away. That was all' (344). Clearly, Katie Donovan errs in asserting that, after her Spanish sojourn, Mary 'returns home to take on her mother's role', and errs again in assuming that Mary will become 'a private exile within her own chosen community' (21). Mary tells us that she will leave both Spain and Mellick.

Rule and convention reassert themselves not only in Mary and Juanito's separation and in Don Pablo's death when he learns of their affair, but also in the character of the salacious, sexually abusive priest, Don Jorge. His priestly status cloaks his corruption; his hood hides his malice from all except his victims. His vituperative account of the 'beautiful young Miss' and Juanito's dance together in the public square mortally wounds Don Pablo. This prurient priest, the only unsympathetic character in the novel, is Kate O'Brien's crude incarnation of society's retaliation for the lovers' indiscretion. All too familiar with the codes by which the Areavagas and Mary live, Don Jorge inflicts society's sentence upon them, and upon Don Pablo, who, although his own man and isolated, nevertheless accepted the old order of his world. That so negative a figure brings so harsh a judgment reinforces Kate O'Brien's view of tradition and morals as more powerful and real than the 'illusion' of romantic love. Social reality triumphs over passion. Although Mary and Juanito break with the conventions of their childhoods in a way that none of Kate O'Brien's earlier characters could have, those conventions overwhelm them in the end.

In its mixture of romantic fantasy and political fact, *Mary Lavelle* belongs to the tradition, established by Charlotte Brontë in *Villette,* of the English ingenue who comes to recognise the depths of her innocence by finding, and then losing, love on the European continent. That earlier work may have been Kate O'Brien's literary model for expressing the emotional and moral repercussions of the choice that leads both her and her heroine far from home. Appropriately, however, *Villette* provides a model that is the very opposite of George Eliot's depiction of regressive loyalty to the known and familiar.

But as a rendering of the social philosophy the author developed during her numerous visits to Spain until the outbreak of the Civil War (when she was barred from entering the country because of her Republican sympathies), *Mary Lavelle* is also directly related to Kate O'Brien's evocative travelogue, *Farewell, Spain.* With one amatory metaphor in *Farewell, Spain,* Kate O'Brien both affirms her equation of Spain with sexual passion and contrasts the familial and familiar affection she feels for Ireland:

Fatal attraction between persons is an old poets' notion that some of us still like to believe is possible and occasional, though not probable — and Spain seems to me to be the *femme fatale* among countries . . . My love has been long and slow — lazy and selfish too, but I know that wherever I go henceforward and whatever I see I shall never again be able to love an earthly scene as I have loved the Spanish. Except some bits of Ireland, bits of home. But that is different. Though Ireland is as beautiful as any country on earth, I am native to her, and therefore cannot feel the novel thrill of her attraction. One does not mix up the love one feels for a parent with the infatuations of adult life. And with Spain I am once and for all infatuated. (227)

In its unusual fusion of the sexual and the national, this passage tells us that Mary's experience at the bullfight and her passion for Juanito are Kate O'Brien's own passion for Spain and for the individuality and personal freedom she found there. The travelogue, written in 1937, a year after the novel, tells of Spain's great reverence for the rights of the individual and respect for his or her idiosyncrasies. Kate O'Brien fears the extermination of these vital human traits by Fascists and Communists alike in the terrible times confronting modern Spain and all of Europe. She describes the Spanish people as both 'profoundly democratic' and 'astoundingly individualistic' (224) — people who bend rules to accommodate their proclivities. Their tumultuous history of 'wars, injustices, miseries, and delays' notwithstanding, the Spanish remain proud and courteous among their compatriots. Respecting their neighbours as they respect themselves, the 'well-bred peoples of this peninsula' have 'none of that "Colonel's lady and Judy O'Grady" *embarras* that still goes on in other quarters of the globe'. Theirs is a 'natural ease which every individual feels in the company of every other' (46). 'Everyone who knows Spain', Kate O'Brien writes,

knows how impressively the man in the street, the reflective middle-aged man in black, can be scrupulous, kindly and understanding towards his neighbour and yet in himself a rock of pride and non-committal gravity. It is their secret to be highly vitalised and yet detached from life. Warm and cold, generous and secretive. (225)

Even as she witnesses the turmoil of contemporary Spain and then hears the deathknell of all that she has come to value most, Kate O'Brien continues to believe that Spain can provide 'some sort of working model of how justice and individualism may flourish together' (225).

But despite her belief in Spain's national resilience and her hope that 'the end of everything decent and lovable is not yet' (225), she writes elegiacally and unashamedly in *Farewell, Spain* 'of that which recedes and is half-remembered. For prophecy and the day ahead', she insists, 'I have no talent and little curiosity. But death and departure attract me as man's brightest hopes have never done' (1). Seeing only monotony immediately before her, Kate O'Brien is an anachronism, the 'sentimental traveller', who writes in praise of 'personal memory, personal love' (6), and insists that 'there is no help for us at all in living through this terrible day, if it takes away our egoists' courage to go on being ourselves' (2). As she waits for a global last gasp, she counts her

ill-starred blessings — the junk we have accumulated and so obstinately loved and sought to increase. Temples, palaces, cathedrals; libraries full of moonshine; pictures to proclaim dead persons, quaint legends, quainter personal conceptions; songs to praise God, or a notion we had that we called by the name of love; tombs and stained-glass windows; symphonies, sonnets, wingless victories — odds and ends of two thousand silly years . . . [of] individualism . . . (5)

In *Farewell, Spain,* Kate O'Brien makes clear that like Don Pablo, she cherishes the Spanish capacity for building a loose 'anarchical system' of government, but, like Juanito, she recognises the current desirability of Communism. 'I am not a Communist', she writes, 'but I believe in the Spanish Republic and its constitution . . . And naturally I believe . . . in the Spanish Republic's right to establish itself communistically, if that is the will of the Spanish people' (123). In *Mary Lavelle* the Areavagas' unfettered social involvement contrasts vividly with the predictable and class-bound attitudes that dominate and control Mary's life — and Kate O'Brien's — in Ireland. In light of that contrast, Kate O'Brien uses Spain's political unrest as the backdrop for her characters' liberation into individual experience.

At the end of Mary's 'lame and helpless story', Kate O'Brien allows her heroine 'only one little, fantastic, impossible hope' (344). Although in *Farewell, Spain,* she expresses this hope politically when she predicts that Fascism and Russian Communism may both fail in Spain, she nevertheless tellingly reiterates her persistent sense of doom when she adds, 'Always assuming, of course — a large assumption — that our modern blustering Caesars can be told in plain language where they get off. Which does not seem possible' (244-5). In *Mary Lavelle,* this gainsaying assumes symbolic expression in the rain that floods the book's conclusion — so unlike the sunlight characteristic of Cabantes, so like the mists of Mellick. Like *Farewell, Spain, Mary Lavelle* is as public and political as it is personal and emotional. Both works eulogise the

individuality that will be lost in Spain; both elegise the personal freedom
that Spain proffered a young, independent Irishwoman.

Five

Pray for the Wanderer

The social theme submerged in the personal story of *Mary Lavelle* moves to the foreground in Kate O'Brien's fourth novel, *Pray for the Wanderer*.[1] Individualism, so powerful in Spain, is once again trapped in Irish tribalism. As hortatory as the hymn from which it takes it name, *Pray for the Wanderer* is more tract than fiction. It condemns the suppression of artistic and individual freedom in the Irish Free State at the expense of literary effectiveness. Although critics of the time praised it, they also noted the novel's excessive social commentary. Evelyn Waugh welcomed the glimpse of the Irish bourgeoisie in a 'book of very high quality', but he remarked that 'Miss O'Brien seems in danger of one of the greatest faults the novelist can commit: of regarding conversations for their general instead of their particular interest ... Her views about modern Ireland are of first-class interest but they are best presented implicitly in the action of her book.'[2]

If *Pray for the Wanderer* fails aesthetically, it is a provocative failure. Written in five months, in contrast to the two or three years[3] Kate O'Brien took to complete her other novels, *Pray for the Wanderer* is most likely, as Vivian Mercier has suggested,[4] a response to the banning of *Mary Lavelle* in 1937 by the Censorship Board of the Irish Free State. In the banning, presumably for the novel's explicit sexual content, Kate O'Brien experienced the humiliating collision of personal statement and public judgment. While *Pray for the Wanderer* voiced her objections to the artistic constraints that the Free State imposed, it satisfied the Censorship Board by extolling and even idealising Ireland's traditional commitment to farm, faith, and family. This pervasive ambivalence splits the novel, complicates its structure, and renders it unique among fiction of the time. Unlike other realistic Irish novels of the 1930s, such as Sean O'Faolain's *Bird Alone* or Frank O'Connor's *The Saint and Mary Kate,* which decry the values of the 'new Ireland', *Pray for the Wanderer* reveres the moral and cultural ethos of the Free State while deploring its manifest social restrictions. It is a forceful reminder of the dilemma of the Irish writer confronting the deepening conservativism of Irish public life.

The geographic and emotional centre of *Pray for the Wanderer* is a

Catholic Big House only moderate in size but ample in comfort. In *Without My Cloak* and *The Ante-Room* such houses belonged to late nineteenth-century Catholic merchants, whose material well-being and nationalistic apathy alienated them from other Irish Catholics as surely as advantage and attitude distanced inhabitants of the Protestant Big House. But in *Pray for the Wanderer,* Weir House is a new version of the Big House, reduced in grandeur and status from all its antecedents, symbolising instead the social and cultural unity of the 1930s. Home to the orthodox values of the recently established State, Weir House is an idealisation of its communal mores — positively prelapsarian in its serenity. 'Life at Weir House', the author tells us, 'was animatedly tranquil . . . Love was the principle' that 'informed' the 'gracious rhythm of [its] days' (94).

But, although Weir House and its inhabitants are cast in a favourable light, Kate O'Brien's central character — a male Irish author, unique in her canon — attacks the popular philosophy they embody. Matt Costello, whose works have been banned in his native land, expresses Kate O'Brien's feelings about a society that muzzles its writers. Nursing a heart broken by Louise Lafleur, the actress who had been his mistress and his muse for two years, Matt comes home to Mellick, seeking solace among the familiar faces and surroundings of his childhood. In at least half the conversations on religion, morality, and politics that comprise *Pray for the Wanderer,* Kate O'Brien decries through Matt the prudery and obscurantism of contemporary Catholic Ireland. But unlike Mary Lavelle, who will lose her place in a world whose innocence is no longer compelling, whose intolerance is all too constricting, whose morality is all too confining, Matt Costello is drawn briefly to the very way of life from which he has so deliberately detached himself. His ambivalence mirrors Kate O'Brien's own.

Eamon de Valera's Constitution of 1937, unveiled as Kate O'Brien worked on *Pray for the Wanderer,* was, in its social dimension, a codification of the Irish Catholic values to which the majority of the population subscribed and which Weir House illustrates. As F.S.L. Lyons has explained, its 'directive principles of social policy' were strictly 'in line with Catholic thinking' and 'corresponded to an ideal with which many Irish men and women would have been in instinctive sympathy'.[5] In the new Constitution, the State 'committed itself publicly to upholding a pattern of life that the majority of its citizens', none more than the occupants of Weir House, 'felt to be the right pattern for them'.[6] So obviously do the inhabitants of Weir house embody the Constitution's social ideals that one wonders whether Kate O'Brien consulted the Articles devoted to the 'fundamental rights' of family, education, private property, and religion as she wrote. The characters in *Pray for the*

Wanderer, among whom de Valera's Constitution is, itself, a frequent subject of discussion, certainly do.

Preoccupied as she is with family life, Kate O'Brien would have been particularly drawn to the assertion in Article 41 of 'the Family as the natural primary and fundamental unit group of society, as a moral institution . . . superior to all positive law'. The hub of Weir House is the family; its heads are Matt's brother, Will, and his wife, Una, who are expecting their sixth child. Kate O'Brien would have been intrigued also by the special place Article 41 accords women in the family and in the state: 'by her life within the home, woman gives to the State a support without which the common good cannot be achieved'.[8] According Una such status at Weir House, Kate O'Brien shows her caring for her home and family with infinite love, patience, and skill, living for others 'as naturally as she [drinks] tea'. Una is no martyr, however; she attends to her own needs as comfortably as she does to her family's. She is the traditional ideal, a wife 'completely subservient' to her husband, 'without once remembering that so she had vowed to be at the altar'. Finely attuned to Will's needs, Una shields him from everyday hurts. 'Her arms are always waiting for him . . . She loves him . . . quite perfectly'. Una is equally loving and sympathetic to her children; she delights in their company. She occasionally loses 'her mild temper' and 'shoos' them away when they pester, but then apologises 'as if she were one of themselves'. Una lives totally in the present. 'Without self-consciousness . . . or even a breath of wonder', she is fulfilled. 'Will and the children used her up, and in so doing vitalized her' (95-8).

The Criminal Law Amendment Act of 1935, banning artificial contraception, must have motivated Una's characterisation.[9] Kate O'Brien's obvious nod here to the Act is at odds with her criticism of large families, suggested by Molly's death in *Without My Cloak*. Her implicit approval of Una, the wife whose 'arms are always waiting' for Will, contrasts markedly with the censuring of conjugal bonds and domesticity in her earlier novels; Kate O'Brien's acceptance testifies to her uncertainty following the censoring of *Mary Lavelle* and to her intention that *Pray for the Wanderer* reflect Ireland's prevailing social ethos.

Will is an Irish Adam to Una's Eve. 'Good and principled', orthodox and traditional, he is imbued with 'a sense of piety to past and future' (97). The notions that happiness can be found outside the family and 'that life might fruitfully be a lonely track or a jealously personal adventure' (3) are foreign to him. Almost as a rebuttal to *Mary Lavelle,* he understands and values only those principles 'founded in family feeling and protected by household gods' (97). Will wonders 'how a man could, or could be glad to circumvent, the blood emotions' (3).

His own life flows from his 'blood channels'; they are his boundaries, 'his circuit, limited but warm' (3). In the naturalness and reciprocal satisfactions of their marriage, Una and Will suggest the idealism behind the edict in Article 41 that 'no law shall be enacted providing for the grant of a dissolution of a marriage'.[10] Affirming the optimism and paternalism behind governmental policy, Kate O'Brien has constructed the archetype of a perfect Irish Catholic marriage: traditional, circumscribed, yet gratifying to both spouses.

In *Pray for the Wanderer,* the vision of a unified nation enhances the harmonious portrait of family life. We are meant to believe that the Costellos, unlike the Considines and Mulqueens of the earlier Mellick novels, share the tenets and concerns of their countrymen. The family's political attitudes create the image of social unity in Ireland. As one might expect, Will, an affluent landowner, supports W.T. Cosgrave as head of the Opposition. He lives as comfortably under de Valera, however, as he did under Cosgrave because, as a dairy farmer, he is immune to de Valera's threat to return grazing land to tillage. 'We dairy farmers are a power in the land now' (46), Will proudly tells his brother. Una, of course, votes with Will, whereas her more modern sister, Nell, supports de Valera. But political differences within the family and, by extension, within Ireland, are congenial because, in Kate O'Brien's interpretation as later in Terence Brown's,[11] the differences in social values under de Valera and under Cosgrave are inconsequential. In *Without My Cloak* and *The Ante-Room,* Kate O'Brien had gently chastised her own class for its distance from the mainstream of Irish life. In *Pray for the Wanderer,* Ireland and Kate O'Brien's milieu are one, and if she lauds both through the family of Weir House, she equally scorns them through Matt. In this novel, Ireland rebuffs only the artist.

Ireland had rebuffed the artist when it rejected *Mary Lavelle,* and in *Pray for the Wanderer,* Kate O'Brien describes her country neither so ideally nor so inaccurately as to overlook its narrowness and repression. Matt Costello enters Mellick's cosy enclave in 1937, no longer a believing Catholic, but an apostle of individual and artistic freedom. Suffering from a 'cosmic conscience', he fears for the future of the 'miserable world' (62-3). In *Pray for the Wanderer* only Matt alludes to the doom that is about to descend on Europe:

nationalisms foaming at the mouth; grown men taking instruction from this little creature or that as to how they shall think; how, or if, they shall pray; how they are to breed, what work they may do, how many rooms they may occupy; what salute they must give to what flag, and what songs they must sing. Abyssinia, China, Spain . . . The same doom awaiting every country in every other country's re-armament intentions. (43)

Matt's fear contrasts with the insularity and complacency in Ireland, which his brother typifies and represents. Isolated, self-satisfied, benign, Will fails to grasp that 'Europe, the Western world was . . . growing tired of what was for him the sweetest natural law. He did not see where the frightened world had got to. He was not frightened. He was a citizen of the Irish Free State, and a family man' (4).

Unlike Will, Matt recognises the onset in Ireland of the mental slavery that is devouring Europe. The censorship of his novels in Ireland expresses the same intolerable disavowal of human rights that prevails in Russia or Germany: 'If you . . . read my books and sit in judgment on them — by what right do you decide that it is not for others to do so? Sheer impertinence' (206). To the charge that his work is 'anti-social, myth-creating and unnecessary', and therefore worthy of censorship, he answers, 'Yes, indeed — and the gods be thanked. So might [it] continue to be while the world remained [a] smug, dead colony of slaves' (91-2).

Individual and artistic freedom is Matt's war cry: 'Man's courageous, individual heart undiscoverable anywhere. Even at last the poets in vocal flight — to absurd and terrible obedience. Hugging their chains. Singing the new theme of captivity'. De Valera is another version of Europe's dictators, and Ireland, 'a dictator's country too' (42). Mellick seems to Matt tragically in goose-step with the rest of Europe.

Ireland's Catholicism is its own brand of fascism; the passivity here bespeaks the loss of individuality on the Continent. The loss, Matt insists, is a 'world disease', expressing itself in Ireland as 'an inflammation of that Jansenism that Maynooth has threatened . . . for so long. Now it's ripee at last — and we're sick like the rest of the world' (80). De Valera 'did not bring materialism out for public adoration', like Stalin, 'but materialistic justice controlled by a dangerous moral philosophy, the new Calvinism of the Roman Catholic Church. That was his rod, his particular bundle of fasces' (43-4).

De Valera wields his power subtly; the Irish Church does not. Matt finds it despicable that the new Constitution has strengthened its dictatorial powers. With a writer's more subtle attention to its language, Matt's reading of the Constitution exposes its manipulation of Irish society; and his opinions clearly mirror Kate O'Brien's:

And now the proffered Constitution of the Irish Free State was before the world. Founded, intelligibly enough and even as this house was, upon the family as social unit, and upon the controlled but inalienable rights of private ownership, but offering in its text curious anomalies and subtleties, alarming signposts. Dedicated to the Holy Trinity . . . but much more in step with the times than was apparent to such men as Will, for instance. Subtle, but dictatorial and obstinate. (44)

Negative manifestations of the power of the Church are visible everywhere: in the censorship of Matt's works, in the bruised hands of Liam, a preposterously obedient child, beaten by his schoolmaster (a priest), and in the rampaging Catholic societies that exercise a malignant, Calvinist form of social control. 'Control! That's where the world's going crazy', Matt says. 'Oh, that most dangerous word "control"! This arrogation of "control" is the darkest and most hideous arrogance! There's doom in it — nothing else!' (202).

But for all his ranting, Matt succumbs to the old, comfortable ways and the old, familiar feelings. As the tolerance and respect for the individual in Spain charmed Mary Lavelle, so Mellick engrosses Matt, and he cannot quite believe that 'this pretty scene of . . . hope, this sample of continuity' has become 'a thing of ruin and archaisms' (42-3). Even as Matt insists that Ireland resembles other European states that uphold *Kinder, Kuchen,* and *Kirchen,* he has a nagging suspicion that her tyranny departs from the general European savagery. Ireland promises, even 'under Dev's tricky constitution' (45), as Matt calls it, a future in such men as his brother Will. Therefore, even as he includes Ireland among those nations in which the light of freedom is waning, Matt praises his brother:

as Sodom and Gomorrah might have been saved by five good men, so perhaps, perhaps the warm personal principle now about to die . . . bitterly wronged sweetness of personal liberty . . . the one good light going out — might yet be saved by a few men of blind good sense who knew not what they did. A few more Wills innocently cultivating their gardens, and the old beaten principle might be accidentally, paradoxically saved . . . (4)

As Matt unearths virtues from his childhood that make even the 'addicted wanderer' (69) cling to home, Weir House becomes 'a shield and a postponement' (29). Longingly, he wonders if he can build a new life in a land where milk has replaced Guinness and Jameson as 'the wine of the country' (46), if, here in the land of his fathers, he can forget the sorrow and the joy of his recent past. He wonders if he can 'live in de Valera's Ireland, where the artistic conscience is ignored', if he can turn 'over a new leaf, turning back to an old . . . and live like the decent son of his father, even the son of his Church, that he waseven the son of his Church, that he was born to be?' (159-60).

Yielding to his native land, in spite of all its 'nonsense and untruth' (159), Matt tries to restructure his life by imagining himself in love with Una's sister, Nell. Nell is the new Irishwoman, accepting all the old social values but expressing them in a modern way. Thirty-three and unmarried, she is not like the dependent spinsters of *Without My Cloak* and *The Ante-Room* nor the Misses of Altorno, lost and unfulfilled;

she is independent and self-supporting, a teacher with a Masters Degree, who lectures on World History in Gaelic. Perfect daughter of the new State, Nell spent summers in the Gaeltacht perfecting her Irish and now speaks it fluently. She smokes, drives her own car, and freely voices her political views. Nell avidly supports de Valera and his policy of providing the 'greatest good for the greatest number'. She despises individualism; 'we should all behave alike and only say what everyone wants to hear'. She believes that 'there are no privileges for anyone', that 'social duty demands certain taboos of speech and action' (91). 'Inclined to admire dictators' (179), she is also profoundly Catholic and active in several societies for the preservation of Catholic values. Matt ironically believes he has found his solace and his solution in her, in 'her beauty, her sanity, her traditional magnificence' (239). He is willing to sacrifice his artistic freedom and individuality for a sheltered life with her:

To pay court to Nell Mahoney was the only real way to say good-bye to all that had happened to him, all that he had built up and sought to make himself . . . He must attempt this most extraordinarily dangerous thing in which every inch would be a battle, every idea a dispute. Success in what he now envisaged would mean a fight for every sentence of his future work, and would even mean the risk of surrender to an entirely new and improbable source of inspiration. (212)

But, approaching Nell, Matt senses what his proposal portends: his life would have to withstand incessant scrutiny, his art survive constant criticism. Kate O'Brien's description of his mood before he asks Nell to marry him tells a predictably destructive tale: 'It is such a sadness as a man feels in the hour before he leaves home for a hospital and an illness, or as may sometimes choke the heart of a child about to return to school after happy holidays. Irrational self-pitying — but deadly sorrow. A farewell heard only by the self. A knowledge of inescapable change' (242).

An inescapable change, indeed, for when Matt proposes, he pledges to comply with the Church and even to censor his own writings. He will have to abide the snobbishness and sophistication that

had produced, but would by no means read *Ulysses* — the most awful outcry ever raised about the powers of darkness . . . A snobbery perilously overnurtured — into cruelty and blindness — by the alarmist policy of the Church, but having, too, its indigent graces, as life at Weir House gave proof . . . But untenable for better or worse by the artist, who can allow himself no snobberies, who can sacrifice his investigations to no policy, whose field is the hidden, the lonely and the individual. (114)

Joyce, most famous and most infamous of the writers banned by the country he rejected, is a touchstone in *Pray for the Wanderer;* Kate O'Brien refers to him several times in the novel. Like Joyce and like Kate O'Brien herself, Matt conducts a love-hate relationship with Ireland, at once railing against the narrow-mindedness that drove him out, yet celebrating the country's time-honoured pleasures:

Roses swooned in beauty on the table; the brood mares and the silver trophies kept their ancient places; beyond the window lay childhood's unchanged garden . . .
    Matt felt a spasm of boredom, almost of outrage. This rounded-off contentment, this imperturbable and well-earned peace! Oh heaven! (308)

Nell saves Matt from further 'boredom and outrage'. She refuses to marry him, even though she is strongly attracted to him, because she knows his love for Louise Lafleur will never die. Louise is his inspiration, 'his greatest creation'; he 'planted' a 'superb conception' on a 'normal and sensible' (263-4) woman so that he could write about her. Nell, however, wants all the love of the man she marries; he may have no other idols, no other models for his devotion. She knows she and Matt are an ill-suited pair.

    Furthermore, Matt has a rival. He must compete with Tom Mahoney, Nell's former fiancé — and her cousin. Nell had broken their engagement when she learned that he had illegitimately fathered a son. Although Tom had been assiduously paternal to the boy, Nell could not accept this breach of conduct. It is Matt's impulsive proposal that ironically reconciles the cousins. Once again, Kate O'Brien has woven a web of unbreakable family ties, the ties that brought Caroline back to Mellick, that drew Agnes to Marie-Rose, that kept Denis at home with Anthony, and had at first attracted Mary to John. And now, the web that had captured Matt rejects him in favour of Tom.

    Tom is a solicitor, the son of an influential widow and a respected member of society. Very much a man of Mellick, he is, nevertheless, its most cynical critic and, as such, seizes the reader's interest and holds it more firmly than any of the other characters in this novel. A voice of objectivity, Tom satirises the hypocrisy of 'decent' Mellick, a town that tolerates two conspicuous brothels but punishes their patrons. Tom contends that Mellick could extend its hypocritical arms even to embrace the censored Matt should he decide to stay. There are, after all,

'lots of smiling virgins . . . whose mothers wouldn't mind.

    . . . You're rich and famous, and you come of well-respected people. Weren't you born and bred here, God help you, child — and all your people before you? And what's all that you get on with but a lot of foolishness? You'd soon grow out of it . . . A nice young wife now is the very thing for you. 'Let copulation thrive'. And before you can remember your last mortal sin you'll be going to Confession every Saturday. (71)

Tom cuts through the sanctimony and self-deception around him. The renewed religiosity of Mellick, he insists, is not a matter of principle, but a means of political advancement. It is simply

a matter of municipal policy now wearing this little button and that little badge, holding a banner here and running to make a retreat there, with Father O'Hegarty warning you kindly about this, and Father O'Hartigan rapping you over the knuckles about that, and Father O'Hanigan running off to talk to the bishop about you! Town Council stuff! Pure jobbery. (73)

Unlike Matt, however, Tom esteems the historical Church as an institution. A non-observer and non-attender, he nevertheless admires it as he admires no other aspect of human organisation. Upholding the 'One, Holy, Catholic and Apostolical', he is confirmed in his belief that 'he will die in the odour of sanctity, fortified by all the rites' (78).

Tom particularly enjoys his philosophic exchanges with the Franciscan monk, Father Malachi, the embodiment of the purest virtues on which the Free State is founded. A thoroughly scrupulous and logical defender of censorship and the Irish way of life, Father Malachi seems not only Kate O'Brien's atonement for her portrait of Don Jorge, the corrupt priest in *Mary Lavelle,* but her intellectual justification for the values Matt attacks. Next to Nell, Father Malachi is the novel's most intelligent exponent of Irish Catholic morality, and, like Nell, he is a potent representation of Kate O'Brien's ambivalence. The discussions between Matt, Tom, and Father Malachi are a thinly veiled version of the argument Kate O'Brien herself holds with the Irish Free State, and if Matt speaks boldly for the author, Father Malachi speaks benignly for Irish code and Catholic creed. The good monk is yet another reminder of Kate O'Brien's wish to be accepted on grounds she deplored by a country she both loved and left.

The job of the writer, Father Malachi says, is to be concerned with 'good and evil', and the work must be judged accordingly. Men like Matt are dangerous 'fellows . . . the instigators and inspirers of egotism, the handers-on of all the romantic individualist nonsense that's made a shambles of the world' (201). Matt responds to the charges, insisting that the writer's 'terms of reference' are 'individual, not an imposed code', and he must not 'moralize' but 'demonstrate', 'recreate life, not as it is . . . but as the peculiarities of [his] vision and desire assume it' (198). Matt's description of his novels describes Kate O'Brien's own:

I take the emotional life of adults for my field . . . Emotional growth — and
decline — is my quarry, and what moves me most to write is a sense of the
chasm that roars between our complicated everyday life and the still more
complicated life of the breast — yes, and the bridges we fling across, and fail
to fling across. (204)

In setting forth the dangers inherent in Matt's art, Father Malachi
rearticulates a view with which we became familiar in *Mary Lavelle.*
Romantic love, he says, is an 'invention — the biggest and most
dangerous invention of you artists. It isn't nature at all. It isn't real.
It's a trick, an imposition, a thing grafted on' (203). The outcome of
Pray for the Wanderer supports Father Malachi's perceptions of Matt
and of romantic love. The substance of Matt's art and life has no place
in Ireland, where love grows naturally from long-standing relationships
and familial bonds, not from stolen moments between strangers. Indeed,
in this book, romantic love is defined as it was in *Mary Lavelle,* as an
illusion, created by the person who experiences it. It has no reality
for anyone else. As Ireland rejected *Mary Lavelle,* so the society depicted
in *Pray for the Wanderer* rejects the feelings to which Mary succumbed.
De Valera's Ireland offers instead the safety of its own illusions.

Kate O'Brien gives voice to those values which deny Matt a place
in Irish society when Tom finally confronts Nell about her relationship
with Matt and expresses his own long-held feelings for her. For all of
Tom's cynicism, his morality is the morality of Mellick and Ireland of
the 1930s, the morality the Constitution sought to preserve. He deplores
the rigid puritanism that once drove him from Nell but, still, he sounds
very much the puritan himself when he sees her in tears after Matt
proposes:

Eleven years ago, standing in this room you called me cad and hypocrite and
low-down heartless cheat. O.K. Since that time your sanctity, your cold-blooded
spinsterish morality and your general, all-around untouchableness, have been
accepted by your intimidated and edified entourage, until hey, presto! a real
profligate comes along, a gentleman from the great world who had long lost
count of his conquests among the virgins, peeresses and courtesans of all the
capitals. The sort of finished article we can't attempt to imitate in Mellick,
naturally . . . It turns out now that the shortest cut to your heart would have
been through the brothels and bedrooms of Europe! (291-2)

As his rage subsides, Tom professes his love once again. He promises
fidelity and permanence; his love has stood the test of time and place.
He will take no other bride, as Matt might. Tom is as undivided in his
affections as Kate O'Brien's idealised Ireland. No artist, he needs no
muse; his love is for a mortal woman and for her corporeal, real self.

Tom wants neither replacements nor medicaments to assuage the hurt he has felt since Nell rejected him.

I have never been vague about the sole desire of my personal life. For better or worse I have never been able to displace the absolute love I once gave to you and which you flung back in my face. I have tried to, but it was honestly impossible. So I shall die a bachelor, leaving no Mahoneys behind me to do filial reverence, because of you, fair cousin. (296)

Nell is all Tom wants: he counters Matt's proposal with one of his own.

Tom is the voice of all that Nell is: the voice of Mellick, her past, her family, her blood. He is the only man Nell can possibly have. Perhaps because Tom seems a bit preposterous discussing Matt with her, pompously commanding her as though he were the head of the family, Nell looks away and responds instead to all the familiar virtues he represents. She 'heard his voice of eleven years ago, and his words, and smiled now a little at the echoes. He was the same. Rich and formal in feeling, very traditional, every inch a man' (299).

Blessing an alliance between cousins that she will enjoin in *The Last of Summer,* Kate O'Brien drives the artist from his homeland once again. Matt is as crushed by Nell's rejection of his love as he was enraged by Ireland's rejection of his work. His departure is marked by the conflict characteristic of *Pray for the Wanderer*. Matt's negative feelings about his country commingle with positive ones that no amount of rejection or neglect can obliterate:

Oh, green and trim Free State! Smug, obstinate, and pertinacious little island, your sins and ignorances are thick upon your face ... But your guilts seem positively innocent, your ignorances are perhaps wisdom when measured against the general European plight. How odd if the distressful country, the isle of Saints and Doctors from which Patrick banished snakes, should prove a last oasis, a floating Lotus Land when the floods rise! (306-7)

Matt leaves his lotus land wistfully, the dams in the outside world about to break. As much as the resemblances he perceives between de Valera and Europe's despots offend him, Matt — as well as his creator — understands the great differences. Deploring the entrenchment of the Church in the Irish State, Matt Costello and Kate O'Brien both know that the 'tricky constitution' they have reviled for its preservation of a Catholic society grants religious freedom not only to Catholics but to Protestants, and, considering its date, most importantly, to Jews. Both know that if de Valera's Ireland condones censorship, it does not condemn difference of opinion. Preserved by the Constitution, Ireland's law courts protect the rights of person and property that the storm of tyranny has destroyed in Europe.

If she sacrifices literary effectiveness to political commentary in *Pray for the Wanderer,* Kate O'Brien's identification with the artist committed to literary vision is intense. For all the safety and comfort in Ireland, Matt cannot stay there and remain a writer. That smug, obstinate island cannot permit him to be himself. He must go off — the wanderer for whom we are asked to pray. There is no going back to Mellick for the individual or the artist.

Six

The Land of Spices

Near the end of her life, Kate O'Brien remarked, 'Joyce was "the great Artist" — there will never be another.'[1] As a devloping writer, she might not have dreamt of rivalling Joyce's brillance, but a literary kinship with the 'great Artist' is manifest in her novels. As upper-middle-class Catholics, both Kate O'Brien and James Joyce were sensitised, if only briefly, to the privileges of that class and, later and more fully, to its disadvantages. Both experienced the dwindling of fortunes and the disintegration of family life; both suffered the pain of public rejection by the country that emotionally possessed them. Such parallels rendered Joyce's writings the model for Kate O'Brien's artistic growth. Just as the censored *Ulysses* haunted *Pray for the Wanderer,* so *A Portrait of the Artist as a Young Man* informs her next novel. *The Land of Spices*[2] is Kate O'Brien's portrait of the artist as a young woman, and is, in its intricate characterisation and sophisticated double plot, one of her most successful novels. Written in 1941, only two years after her least artistically successful work, *The Land of Spices* reveals Kate O'Brien's mastery of her craft and themes.

In *A Portrait of the Artist as a Young Man,* Joyce returned to Clongowes and Belvedere, the Jesuit schools of his youth. So too, does Kate O'Brien, in her most demonstrably autobiographical work, revisit Limerick's Laurel Hill Convent to which her family had sent her at the age of five, when her mother died. *The Land of Spices* delicately weaves together the stories of Mère Marie-Hélène, the English Reverend Mother at the *Couvent de la Compagnie de la Sainte Famille,* a French order of nuns in Mellick, and Anna Murphy, one of her pupils. Like Stephen Dedalus, Anna is a partial self-portrait of the author, 'a quiet, reflective child, hardworking and bright'.[3] Convent scenes such as the strivings of awkward adolescents for *'la pudeur* and *la politesse',* the bickering and petty cruelties, the *Schwärmerei* of younger pupils for older beautiful girls, and the infectious ecstasy of teen-aged females at the sight of a handsome young cleric, have the clarity of recollection of one who has lived that life.

'Memories of a Catholic Education', a recently published fragment from Kate O'Brien's unfinished autobiography, implies how strongly

Mère Marie-Hélène resembles Reverend Mother of Laurel Hill, whom a very young Kate O'Brien watched 'with respectful attention and grew most affectionately interested in'.[4] In *The Land of Spices,* Kate O'Brien idealises Mère Marie-Hélène, forgoing many of Reverend Mother's less agreeable traits. Nevertheless, Mère Marie-Hélène's origins lie conspicuously in Laurel Hill's 'wise and considerate' if 'cold' and 'inexpressive' nun, who was in strict 'outer command' of her body, yet never 'in command of her little claw hands'. Although Reverend Mother opposed the goals of the Gaelic Revival, this 'just and eccentric governor' allowed enthusiastic nuns 'evening classes and all the books they wanted' as well as 'teaching and direction' in the Irish language. Mère Marie-Hélène's attitudes toward the Irish hierarchy are born of both the antipathy and the respect between Reverend Mother and Edward Thomas O'Dwyer, 'Limerick's very intelligent and arrogant bishop'. Mère Marie-Hélène's small but significant kindness — a bit of sugar at the bottom of a teacup during Lent, for example — were the very ones to which Reverend Mother treated her Laurel Hill students.[5]

Endowing her character with qualities of her own Aunt Mary, the Mother Superior at Presentation Convent,[6] Kate O'Brien transforms this replica of 'Queen Victoria in miniature',[7] into a tall, elegantly beautiful woman, whose decision to become a religious and whose life, in general, are probably as disparate from Reverend Mother's upper-class English reality as is her appearance. The story of Mère Marie-Hélène and the disintegration of her family life is one we recognise as peculiarly Kate O'Brien's, not in its particulars, but in its general pattern . . . of repression and disappointment. Mère Marie-Hélène's history and profile, along with Anna Murphy's, express Kate O'Brien's interest not only in artistic growth, but also in the mysterious effects of family life on the individual. The 'confusions created by parents for children are the most deep and dark of all', says Mère Marie-Hélène, 'the relationship of parent and child is grievously important' (80).

In *A Portrait of the Artist as a Young Man* Stephen Dedalus had argued the artist's need to liberate himself from religion, nation, and family. In *The Land of Spices* Kate O'Brien considers these forces in Irish life during roughly the same historical period, but she presents them more compassionately, within the context of the Irish Catholicism of her youth. *La Compagnie de Sainte Famille* is not perfect, however. Like Joyce, Kate O'Brien shows the cruelty of some members of the Catholic hierarchy; Clongowes's Father Dolan meets his match in *Sainte Famille's* Mother Mary Andrew. Kate O'Brien reveals an arrogance and fatuity within convent walls that seem hardly different from the trivial ways without. Like members of a family, the nuns compete with, control, and manipulate each other, play favourites among the pupils, and indulge their vengeances. Nevertheless, Mère Marie-Hélène is unfailingly wise and just to all 'her girls'. The Bishop, with whom she continually spars over the place of nationalism in Irish education, respects the students, supports women's education, and will unwittingly ally with Mère Marie-Hélène in her campaign for Anna's education.

Thus, although *The Land of Spices* has its share of clerical savagery, Kate O'Brien examines the growth of an aesthetically sensitive young woman under essentially benign religious guidance. In Joyce's *A Portrait of the Artist as a Young Man,* the Church is death; in Kate O'Brien's novel it is life — a privileged life that compensates for worldly sorrows. In contrast to the death's heads and gallows that accompany Joyce's priests, or the ever-present dampness and cold at Clongowes, the Mellick convent and its surroundings are lush and vivifying. The serenity reflects the convent's treatment of its charges, for the most part, free of the rancour that flows between the Jesuits and their students in Joyce's *Portrait.*

Similarly, Kate O'Brien presents the force of Irish nationalism from a more positive perspective than Joyce's. Returning to the time of her youth, she gains the distance to observe more equanimically the Irish chauvinism with which she struggled in *Pray for the Wanderer.* The first of Kate O'Brien's central characters who is not Irish, Mère Marie-Hélène brings an outsider's perspective to the peculiarities of the Irish scene. She is an uneasy protagonist. In nationalist Ireland of 1914, the Ireland of a resurgent Home Rule Party and Gaelic League, there is little place for an Englishwoman. Describing the anomalous position of Reverend Mother at Laurel Hill, Kate O'Brien writes, 'Over the long view one has seen how absurd it was that that little Englishwoman . . . should have been in charge of the education of Irish girls of the Catholic middle class in the years so quickly leading up to 1916'.[8] Mère Marie-Hélène's introduction to this country and its politics, her aversion to its culture and clergy, express Kate O'Brien's negativity towards Ireland. Mère Marie-Hélène refutes Ireland's 'sacred egoism'[9] with its notion that what is good for Ireland is what is good. Despite having actively supported the nationalist movement and avidly studied Gaelic at Laurel Hill, Kate O'Brien presents as both legitimate and objective Mère Marie-Hélène's criticism of this theory, based, the 'Memories' suggests, on the English Reverend Mother's observations. But she grants the nationalists a voice, and they justify their self-absorbed concerns in equally sympathetic tones. The result is a particularly balanced view of the Irish and their political attitudes during this historic period. It is a dual perspective, not unlike that of *Pray for the Wanderer,* but marked less by the polemical ambivalence that pervades that novel than by a desire to present both sides fairly.

Indeed, if there is any suggestion in *The Land of Spices* that Kate O'Brien intends her judgment of Irish nationalistic attitudes to be negative — as she does in her next novel *The Last of Summer* — it lies unobtrusively in the date she chose for its conclusion. She completed the novel in September, 1940; its action ends in June, 1914. The doom awaiting Mère Marie-Hélène's beloved Belgium parallels the horror engulfing Europe as Kate O'Brien wrote. Through Mère Marie-Hélène she deplores the parochial Irish nationalism prevalent in both 1914 and 1940 and, by implication, condemns the self-containment and protectionism rampant in both eras. The dramatisation of the conflict between European tradition and Irish nationalism in the years before the outbreak of World War I conveys the author's anguish over Ireland's declared position in both world wars. During the Great War, with Home Rule in suspension, the Irish did little to help the war effort; they violently opposed conscription and were hardly 'disposed to take an active interest in the fate of Belgium when their own future still seemed so obscure'.[10] Events in Europe, they said, were not Ireland's affair. They remained equally detached throughout World War II when, despite intense pressure from England and America, they 'supported neutrality as the only sane policy in a world gone mad'.[11] Furthermore, the country was united behind de Valera's stance that neutrality was the ultimate test of the young nation's independence. The provincialism that Kate O'Brien attacked in *Pray for the Wanderer* and *The Last of Summer* is present in *The Land of Spices,* but her criticism is muted and oblique.

Although in *The Land of Spices* Kate O'Brien is kinder to Irish nationalism and Catholicism than was Joyce, her view of family life may be even more devastating than his, perhaps because she treats her characters without his irony. The families of this novel suffer more than any in her earlier novels. The central characters of *Without My Cloak* and *The Ante-Room* pay tribute, happily or not, to the primacy of the family. Their counterparts in *Mary Lavelle* and *Pray for the Wanderer,* stifled by their 'blood emotions', sever themselves from their families and cultures to pursue their illusions of romantic love and their dreams of personal freedom. In *The Land of Spices,* however, family ties are more than simply limiting; they are the source of unbearable pain. It is as if, having freed her characters and set them adrift, as she did in *Mary Lavelle* and *Pray for the Wanderer,* Kate O'Brien can now cast a more objective eye on what they left behind, turning innuendo into assertion. The implications that Anthony Considine's possessiveness might harm his son, and that Agnes might suffocate emotionally from confinement in the Mulqueen household, become explicit in the parent-induced pain that Helen Archer, who later becomes Mère Marie-Hélène, and Anna Murphy endure. Family solidarity, strife-ridden but assured in *Without My Cloak* and *The Ante-Room,* is shattered in *The Land of Spices.*

But in this novel, we also witness the processes that salve the characters' wounds. As Stepehen Dedalus's imagination promised him release from the 'nets' of Irish life, so do literature, religion, and a distant, yet shared, love, enable Anna Murphy and Mère Marie-Hélène to withstand and finally accept the losses they have endured. Matt Costello's second departure from his family, from Weir House, and from Ireland solicited the reader's prayer. *The Land of Spices* makes no such demands. Having left their families, Mère Marie-Hélène and Anna find new roots at *Sainte Famille,* their 'land of spices'. The convent school becomes for them a substitute home in which children can sustain the loss of parents or siblings, celibates can adopt children, and, most important, foundering individuals can recover or discover themselves.

Other writers might have granted their characters romantic love as a satisfying replacement for the comforts of family life. But, as Kate O'Brien has already argued, romantic love is an illusion with neither strength nor substance. In *The Land of Spices,* she portrays a variety of loves: between parents and children, between siblings, between nuns, between teachers and pupils, but none between adult heterosexuals. Kate O'Brien explores alternatives to familial bonding through the lives, both individual and shared, of the religious and the artist.

Although in *Pray for the Wanderer* all the characters except Matt see the stability of the individual and of the State as wedded to the stability of the family, Kate O'Brien, nevertheless, sets forth in that novel the religious and artistic alternatives to family life. Will Costello cannot comprehend that, as an artist, his brother Matt must exist without establishing himself 'in piety among his natural household gods'. In Will's limited view, there is no place for Stephen Dedalus's priest of the imagination, who serves neither home, nor Church, nor fatherland. In the character of Anna Murphy, Kate O'Brien shows the youthful inclination towards what is to Will the unacceptable choice his brother has made: art over family and Church. In *The Land of Spices,* Kate O'Brien also explores the other path, that 'mysterious imperative' that Will believes is the only alternative to the perpetuation of the 'blood channels', the religious life. Helen's decision to enter the convent, to live an independent, yet rooted, way of life, both demands and allows circumvention of the 'blood emotions'.[12]

As the novel opens, Mère Marie-Hélène feels incapable of continuing as the English governor of Irish nuns in a French religious order and seeks release. She is increasingly uncomfortable with the Irish people and, particularly, with the intensity of their nationalist views. Her problem is acute because Father Conroy, the young chaplain to *Sainte*

Famille, resents the 'training of Irish girls as suitable wives for English Majors and Colonial Governors!' (92). (Kate O'Brien tells us in 'Memories of A Catholic Education' that Laurel Hill Convent had been accused of the same thing.)

The local Bishop, 'a forthright and progressive man' (14), agrees with Father Conroy that Ireland needs a form of education that will establish a national character and teach her children not merely to feel an 'ancient national grievance, but see why it *is* a grievance, see its cultural and historic reality' (15). The lack of such a curriculum at *Sainte Famille* nettles His Lordship. He chafes at Mère Marie-Hélène's Englishness, her insistence on teaching in the European tradition, and the autonomy of her order. 'Irish national life', he contends, 'is bound up with its religion, and it may well be that educational work will become difficult here soon for those Orders which adhere too closely to a foreign tradition' (15). The Irish hierarchy has no power to counsel, control, or direct the house of an independent religious order, and it deeply resents Mère Marie-Hélène's claim that *Sainte Famille* is not 'a nation' (15), that its business is not with national matters. Thus she remains at a disquieting distance, independent from Father Conroy and the Bishop, despite the latter's personal respect for her. The prelates accuse this 'cold English fish' (13) of not understanding the Irish 'at all, at all' (17). She fears that they are right.

Misunderstood and out of place in Ireland, Mère Marie-Hélène is about to ask for a transfer when the six-year-old Anna Murphy comes to *Sainte Famille* and, like Stephen Dedalus, and perhaps like Kate O'Brien herself, becomes its youngest pupil. Anna must be given refuge from the tormented family that should have protected her. Her father is profligate, a drinker and philanderer, whose most recent conquest was the children's governess. Mrs. Murphy, no longer able to cope with him and adequately attend to her children, places Anna in *Sainte Famille,* the school which she and her own mother had attended. Anna's deep love for her parents, founded in stability and permanence, heightens the injustice in sending so young a child from home. Initially, her father can reassure her that home is 'still real and near her, and anytime she felt it must be so, her daddy would take her back there and let her stay' (49-50).

But home is precious to Anna mostly because her younger brother Charlie is there; they are constant, 'very peaceful friends' (115). For a time, the contentment that envelops Anna when she is with Charlie staves off both her awareness of her family's deterioration and her loneliness at school. After vacations, she can run 'back into school-life feeling exhilarated' only because she is 'fully fed of secure affection for Charlie and for Castle Tory' (116). But her parents' increasingly ferocious arguments greatly upset her. Not even Charlie can deflect their unpleasantness or rouse her former sense of security.

Mère Marie-Hélène empathises with Anna. 'To be forced, when so small, to become one of a large, alien body, merely because parents had neither the sense nor the sensitiveness to keep a child at home' (80) is pathetic. She, too, knows the discomfort of being an outsider. It stung her first when she was eighteen. Until then, as Helen Archer, she had shared with her father a tranquil life that had seemed an intellectual and emotional ideal. A Cambridge-educated authority on English metaphysical poetry and now a teacher in Brussels, her father had once seemed to Helen all that was good and perfect in the world. The harmony between parent and child is reminiscent of Don Pablo and Juanito Areavaga, and, to a degree, of Denis and Anthony Considine. Like Denis and Juanito, Helen was the centre of her father's life (her mother, to whom she had never felt close, had died when she was twelve). Professor Archer educated his daughter and taught her the poetry he cherished — George Herbert's 'Prayer' lends the novel its suggestive title. Helen's pleasure in being with her father was equally intense; it transcended normal filial feeling. She felt for him as Anthony Considine felt for his son, as she might later have felt for a lover.

Kate O'Brien withholds from the reader until the novel's very centre the crisis that destroyed Helen's relationship with her father. Disconsolate when she discovers that he is homosexual, Helen flees her home to the order of *Sainte Famille*. Sickened by him who had seemed perfection itself, she can only ask if this is 'what lay around, under love, under beauty... the flesh they preached about, the extremity of what the sin of the flesh might be' (159). With a containment and control bordering on madness, she reveals to no one, not teacher, friend, or confessor, what she has witnessed or the torment it has caused. She faces the terror of betrayal alone and steers herself 'for ever', she believes, from 'the devilry of human love' (159). Helen Archer becomes a nun, then, not as a saintly act of self-denial, but as a desperate escape from pain. The convent school in Brussels having presented a vocation as the only rival to her father's perfection, Helen chooses the religious life ineluctably. When she was a young girl considering the ideals of family feeling and religious devotion, 'all her *feelings* gave victory to him'; now, what was formerly 'only an intellectual temptation' (155), has become the only substitute for her emotionally satisfying life with her father.

In *A Portrait of the Artist as a Young Man*, the religious life experienced by Stephen Dedalus at the Jesuit schools of Joyce's youth appears as both a promise and a threat. It must be rejected if creativity is to thrive. In Joyce's writing, unlike Kate O'Brien's, the Church offers no relief from the deprivations of family life; rather, it emerges as equally noxious to the creative spirit. In *A Portrait of the Artist as a Young Man,* family and religion both bruise the artistic sensibility. In *The Land of Spices,* however, as in the later *The Last of Summer* and *The Flower of May,* conventual life fosters love and creativity. These novels suggest that, like Joyce, Kate O'Brien may have been tempted by the religious life, and although she, too, resisted the temptation, her Laurel Hill schooling remained a benign but powerful force in her artistic development.

In *La Couvent de la Compagnie de la Sainte Famille* (the name Kate O'Brien gives the order is surely not coincidental), keeping 'her life serenely at His disposal' (18), Helen grows professionally and spiritually. She becomes a competent nun. But, despite her intelligence and ability, she tries to deny love's existence; God becomes 'equity, detachment, justice, purity — anything good that was not love. Anything good that was cold and had definition' (28). When, at the age of thirty, she is recalled to the Mother House, not far from her father's home in Brussels, she dreads returning to that place where all her past is 'fixed in the hurtful, clear light of remembrance'. Once 'a little girl's world of everyday sounds and smells', it is now 'the container' of 'too sudden injury', of 'crippling and panic' (19). Helen's dread suggests the complex feelings that led to Kate O'Brien's many years in self-imposed exile. Ireland surely held for the author a share of remembrances as tender and agonising as Helen Archer's.

Perhaps writing through her own taut attachments to home and family, Kate O'Brien allows Mère Marie-Hélène the surprising discovery that she can again receive her father's love. She has learned, through her vocation, to accept human frailty, athough, until now, only 'in theory and at a remove' (20). Her wound begins to heal as she recognises that her earlier love for her father, so vulnerable to the knowledge of his weakness, had been nothing more than 'fatuous egotism' (20). With the scrupulously honest and critical self-observation of Kate O'Brien's strongest heroines, she sees her vengeance of eleven years, her flight from her father into the convent, as 'stupidity masquerading offensively before the good God'. Now her duty is 'to stand still and eventually understand' (20). Yet, with all her forgiveness, she cannot imagine ever being completely free of the agony her father has caused her: 'she had worshipped as perfect the author of her disillusion . . . the blow had been agonising pain', and despite all the change in her feelings, 'would indeed always leave her limping, no matter how she strove with wisdom' (20).

Soon, however, Mère Marie-Hélène is sent, for political reasons within the Order, to become Reverend Mother of the convent in Mellick. There, in her confrontations with the Irish, she loses the generosity of spirit she felt for her father. Her soul withers, her humanity dissolves, and, having known the fullness of human acceptance, she cannot tolerate losing it again. Her wish to return to Brussels is a wish to flee the antipathy she has come to despise in herself.

Anna's chance recitation of 'Peace', the poem by Henry Vaughan that Mère Marie-Hélène's father had loved and taught her, provokes the nun to re-address her feelings and her wish to leave Ireland. Having forgiven her father, she feels the need to forgive, the obligation to care for, all human weakness. Anna is the vehicle by which Mère Marie-Hélène continues her journey towards her fullest self, towards the joy of her emotions and the exaltation of human life. The recitation reawakens the compassion that will direct Mère Marie-Hélène both to her father and to her future. In Anna's little voice she hears 'her own young nights of uncomforted sobbing, and saw and felt once more, within her own far-away experience, the dark convulsions and intersection of the paths that lead innocence to knowledge and desire and dream to reality' (82). Poetry sustains them both, and their shared love of literature binds student to teacher. Anna's weekly recitations, at Mère Marie-Hélène's request, reinforce the nun's purpose and the child's literary predisposition.

But literature is not merely Anna's delight, it is also her retreat. Even Mère Marie-Hélène is powerless to spare her from Mother Scholastic's resentment of her academic achievements and the damage it inflicts on her soul. As Father Dolan's brutality taught Stephen Dedalus the arbitrary power of authority, arousing in him the desire to fight it, so Mother Mary Andrew's cruelty teaches Anna 'her first contempt for a fellow creature' (110). Driven by disappointment and a 'shock to her confidence' (112), Anna withdraws from those around her and becomes an avid reader, one 'who will gratefully read anything rather than not read' (112). Her 'random and uncritical hobby', made her 'formidable and annoying in class' and 'held her back somewhat from normal friendships' (114).

These first signs of Anna's literary proclivity may reflect Kate O'Brien's experience, but they also owe a great deal to Joyce's description of Stephen Dedalus. As a very young girl, Anna was as fascinated with words as Stephen was. 'Words, their shapes and lengths, their possibilities of breaking into other words, or into pairs and groups of letters, became her constant amusement' (112). Kate O'Brien's depiction of Anna's word-playing is filled with Joycean echoes:

She liked to shut her eyes and wonder why 'yellow' was dove-grey, and why 'black' was flaming orange. She tried in vain to turn them to other colours. Long words were like striped ribbons — 'constitution', for instance, was scarlet, white, blue, black across its flashing syllables. The best long words broke up into groups of three letters, leaving no tail; the next best went in twos; words of eleven letters were ugly-looking, disappointing. (112-13).

Like Joyce's young writer, Anna ponders the connection between the sounds of words and their meanings: *'Ainsi soit-il* — there it was again — a very bright sound, like a bugle in the street' (34). She revels even in the sounds of words she does not understand. Listening to a German recitation of Schiller, she finds shapes and meanings in the sounds of his language: 'beyond her present recognition, a vista of wide, starry melancholy, a measured mournful panorama of she knew not what, of evocations, intimations, images — the floating formal beauty of suggestive words. Very sad, very shapely on the air' (181). Like Stephen, Anna responds to the sounds of Schiller's words without being trapped by their meanings.

Words are as tactile to Anna and to Stephen as the physical realities of the world around them. Her thoughts recapture the rhythms as well as the substance of his musings:

No cross, no crown. He sees your sacrifice. Anna leant contentedly on the window-ledge; the women's talk flowed in dark shapes that interested her. The brilliant symbols, Cross and Crown, wound variously in pursuit of each other, in escape, through velvet darkness; the deep word 'sacrifice', the solemn 'He', marked time. It was grandiose, it made her dreamy, and it was familiar. Grandmother said that too — no cross, no crown. It was a musical thing to say. (40)

But Anna's aesthetic development is arrested and Mère Marie-Hélène is thrust once more into the pain of her past when each loses to death the person she loves most: Mère Marie-Hélène, her father, and Anna, her brother. Deftly manipulating plot and character, Kate O'Brien reveals now, upon Professor Archer's death at the midpoint of the novel, the trauma to which Helen had been subjected years earlier. The reader's shock replicates Helen's upon finding her father and his student Etienne 'in the embrace of love' (157). (It was this euphemistic phrase that caused the Irish Free State to censor the novel.) A literary *tour de force,* Kate O'Brien's use of suspense in *The Land of Spices* demonstrates, as did the adroit compression of *The Ante-Room* into three days of religious solemnity, her skill as a story-teller.

When Mère Marie-Hélène learns that her father is dying, she kneels 'immobile and seeking grace, all night, before her memories of him' (145), reliving her past. Her heart softened by her love for Anna, Mère Marie-Hélène accepts her father's weakness fully and finally. She knows that in the eyes of the Church he is a sinner, but she sees 'her own sin of arrogant judgment as the greater', recognising 'its insolence, not merely against God but against His creature' (160). In a moving *double entendre* she prays:

'Father, forgive me — I know not what I did'.

She repeated the prayer. In her weariness she did not know whether she addressed it to Heaven or to her earthly father, whom now again at the eleventh hour she beheld, and felt in her heart with sudden sweetness, as he had been to her in childhood. (160)

At last, without anger or prejudice, relieved in the knowledge that he died devoid of 'all the woe and pain that lay between them' (164), Mère Marie-Hélène, limping no longer, can pray 'humbly for her father's waiting soul' (161).

Kate O'Brien maintains the carefully controlled parallelism of her two main characters; Anna, too, suffers a profound trauma that impedes her literary growth. She loses the joys of childhood and family, at first intermittently, with her parents' incessant arguing, and then irrevocably with the drowning of her beloved Charlie, a loss that affects Anna as acutely as Professor Archer's homosexuality affected Helen. Mr Murphy's drunkenness and the domestic strife at Castle Tory intrude on Anna's visits home, despite the joy that Charlie brings her. In her early teens, Anna must address 'anxieties she did not often try to formulate because . . . she still needed very much — since she was lonely at school — to feel her parents as her protectors and as the source of warm safety' (172), but at Castle Tory, 'life too often now came menacingly near, looking sad and intractable' (172). Finally, Anna must confront her family's instability with wide-open, adolescent eyes. When dwindling fortunes threaten to cancel the Murphys' cherished summer holiday at Doon Point, her awareness of adult cruelty and pain overtakes childhood innocence. 'For the first time she felt that Doon Point too was subject to . . . the undefined yet increasingly perceptible sadnesses of life beyond childhood, the changes and shadows that darkened older faces, and made so much uncertain that once was sure' (196). Anna fears that the decline of the Murphys' finances and security will inevitably affect her destiny. Personal freedom is 'expensive' and what was done for her elder brothers might not be done for her. 'If a girl sees liberty as the greatest of all desirables', as Anna does, 'she will have to spin it out of herself, as the spider its web' (199).

As independence beckons her, Anna imagines herself not as a wife or mother, or even, with any constancy, a nun. Rather, she delights in projecting herself into dominant, masculine roles: a leader of brave fishermen, an explorer in Antarctica, an Irish national leader, or a humble and handsome Canadian 'Mountie'. As she fantasises, Anna, however, acknowledges the obstacles in her way:

She wanted time, and secrecy, and no interference and no advice ... she was both cunning and realistic ... What you had to do was to play for time. You wanted none of the lives you saw about you, and at present saw no way to any other. But the thing was to keep your head, to be still and watchful, and walk into no traps. (207-8)

Kate O'Brien echoes Joyce to indicate that Anna will follow Stephen's path. Although she is not yet fully conscious that her destiny is as a writer, Anna sounds very much like Stephen Dedalus when he realises that his personal and aesthetic survival will require 'silence, exile, and cunning'.

In 1914, however, higher education and career were neither the norms nor the rights of young Irish women, even of upper-middle-class women. The course Anna has set will not be easy. She wants nothing of the lives of the women around her — among women only Mrs Pankhurst piques her interest — but, as yet, she sees no other way open to her. The feminist themes implicit in Kate O'Brien's earlier novels, women's social entrapment in *Without My Cloak* and *The Ante-Room,* their struggle for independence in *Mary Lavelle* and in the character of Nell in *Pray for the Wanderer,* are more explicit in *The Land of Spices.* In this book, women sustain women: nuns sustain each other and the girls in their charge; the girls support each other. Anna Murphy, unwittingly, supports a nun. Even Anna's awareness of her artistic potential comes to her in female form. The introduction, late in the novel, of Miss Robertson, a once-jailed suffragist, brings the feminist theme closer to the surface. Miss Robertson befriends Anna at Doon Point just before Charlie dies, and her questioning about Anna's future causes the girl's 'heart' to thud 'uneasily' (207). Arguing with the Bishop about women's rights and about the narrowness of Irish nationalist politics, Miss Robertson presages the struggle Anna will face as a female writer.

Charlie's death is the end of Anna's innocence. Unlike Anna's mother, who is so caught up in her hostilities that she can barely intimate maternal feeling, Mère Marie-Hélène cautiously helps Anna weather her crisis. One conversation, in particular, is an ironic reminder of Stephen's visit to the rector to protest against Father Dolan's harsh treatment: 'I am at your disposition — because we are both, you for the time being and I for life, members of *Sainte Famille* ... and I, for my part, have always been fonder of you than of other pupils. Perhaps because you were such a baby when you came' (239)

But even after the storm of Charlie's death, Mère Marie-Hélène continues to be involved in Anna's life. She confronts the girl's too pious, controlling grandmother, who, although Anna has won a highly competitive national scholarship, refuses to support her wish to attend university as her brothers had. Using the old woman's self-importance to manipulate the argument on Anna's behalf, Mère Marie-Hélène insists that education is Anna's right. There are no strings attached to Mère Marie-Hélène's intervention; Anna is free to leave *Sainte Famille* without even the insinuation that she must be a nun — and Anna asserts that she will not come back to wear the holy habit.

At liberty to pursue her education, Anna experiences an epiphany. The climactic moment is cast, not surprisingly, in another Joycean mould: like Stephen, Anna sees herself an artist. Pilar, a classmate, asks Anna to help her understand Milton's 'Lycidas'. Since Charlie's death, Anna had been unable to read Milton's elegy, wincing if ever she came across it. But now, approached by the beautiful Pilar on a warm summer evening, she finds in Milton's lines the artistic expression of a sorrow very much like her own. Anna cannot clarify the poem's meaning for Pilar, yet she finds in 'the elegiac composure of the lines' (270-71) a powerful deliverance from her grief. Free to create, Anna transforms Pilar into a work of art, much as Stephen shaped the girl on the beach into a beautiful sea bird. Pilar's aesthetic beatification is redolent of Joyce; she represents to Anna what the girl represented to Stephen. Anna saw her as 'a symbol as complicated as any imaginative struggle in verse; a common piece of creation, an exquisite challenge to creativeness; she saw Pilar as a glimpse, as if she were a line from a lost immortal; she saw her ironically, delightedly, as a motive in art' (271-2).

Like Stephen, Anna becomes aware of her artistic potential in an emblem of mortal beauty. Pilar is living proof that poets' lines lie in the commonplaces of life; she has the 'power to make life compose around' her (272). Anna does not understand fully the 'translation of the ordinary' (272) she has witnessed, but she grasps its import. She can 'only accept it and wait; but her heart leaped premonitorily' (272). Here again, Kate O'Brien's two plots reflect each other, for Pilar has affected Anna as Anna has affected Mère Marie-Hélène, liberating her from the past and her pain. A female Stephen Dedalus about to 'fly by those nets' that confine her, Anna is ready to become an artist, recreating 'life out of life'.[13]

For Anna, as for Mère Marie-Hélène, *Sainte Famille* has been a second family, a holy, human family, that will send her steadily, if timidly, on her way. In the nun's parting words to Anna, Kate O'Brien depicts a surrogate parent who deeply loves her child, and yet, unlike Anthony Considine, can let her go: 'You have been my very dear child, and you will always be that, to the end of my life. Run on now, and God bless you' (284).

But Anna is not the only one who will leave *Sainte Famille* for a new and unknown life. At the novel's end, Mère Marie-Hélène has been given the order's supreme honour; she has been elected to the post of Mère

Générale and must return to Brussels. Her leave-taking is difficult, for after years of travail, she now readily admits that Ireland is 'very beautiful', sometimes even 'holy for a minute — an island *for* if not *of* saints' (283). Furthermore, 'shadows of evil and danger were indeed gathering' abroad. 'Germany, Austria, the Balkans, all were seething . . . No one could guess how war would come to Europe, but only that it was visibly on its way' (279). Mère Marie-Hélène, however, finds strength for her mission in its source: 'the training of the Christian mind would go on . . . however many wars barbarians wage. And indeed *Place des Ormes* seemed as peaceful a corner in Europe now from which to promote the glory of God' (279). Ironically, there will be no peace. In Belgium, Mère Marie-Hélène will face the destruction of all she had known of goodness and beauty in the world. But, like Anna, listening with the 'pain of premonition' (215) to a band of Germans playing *'Die Lorelei'* at Doon Point, or Charlie singing it to the seals before he drowns, Mère Marie-Hélène has found beauty and love before the deluge.

Seven

The Last of Summer

The Last of Summer[1] is a synthesis of Kate O'Brien's earlier novels. Again, amid all the elements of the Irish Catholic upper-middle class, the author asserts that deep, instant love must submit to family and culture. Yet the overall effect of *The Last of Summer* is very different. Antipathy replaces the ambivalence that, until *The Land of Spices,* had marked her treatment of both family life and Irish tenets. In her most explicitly Freudian novel to date, Kate O'Brien presents mother/son affection, the personification of her relationship with her motherland, as overtly pathological. In *The Last of Summer,* her lovers are each involved in the romance of parental love from which only one escapes. Equating Irish political insularity with family life, Kate O'Brien uses these damaging, unresolved oedipal conflicts to symbolise Ireland's distance from the larger European scene. Ireland's neutrality appears as immoral isolationism in political terms, and pathetic self-absorption in human terms.

In 1943, two years after *The Land of Spices* met with native disfavour, Kate O'Brien condemns not only the Irish bourgeoisie of her childhood, but the country as a whole. Her denunciation must be attributed in part to the banning of *The Land of Spices* by the Irish Censorship Board. In *Pray for the Wanderer,* Kate O'Brien expressed her ambivalence towards the censoring of *Mary Lavelle,* criticising the Board's action and the national attitudes that triggered it, but, at the same time, implying that she could write fiction the Board would accept. *Pray for the Wanderer* castigated de Valera's Ireland as it eulogised the country's simple, shielded comforts. But the censoring of *The Land of Spices,* a novel that has none of the explicit sensuality of *Mary Lavelle,* and portrays, rather than a heterosexual relationship, a nun's love for her father and for a young student, seems to have drained Kate O'Brien of that ambivalence. The latent fury in *The Last of Summer* suggests that, having condoned the Ireland of her youth in *The Land of Spices,* she was deeply wounded by her contemporaries' reprobation. She condemns the attitudes responsible; bitterness, more than nostalgia, suffuses *The Last of Summer.* The novel conveys Kate O'Brien's distress that her books could not go home again. It is not surprising that she will set *That Lady,* her next novel, in sixteenth-century Spain, finding geographic and temporal distance from Ireland in a country that, until only recently, had been most hospitable.

The Last of Summer, like *Pray for the Wanderer,* is less successful than the novel it implicitly defends. The characterisations that make *The Land of Spices* so effective are far less subtle here, even strident, yet *The Last of Summer* is not without appeal. Indeed, such is her skill that Kate O'Brien can make both provocative and vital what appears on the surface a textbook oedipal relationship and a crude allegory of national idiosyncrasies. Although anger seems to have forced the author's hand to bolder strokes, the characters in *The Last of Summer* are believable and compelling, and their stories — both personal and political — mesh well with what we know of Ireland in the late 1930s and early 1940s.

In *The Last of Summer,* her family's history again provides the source for Kate O'Brien's story — that of a spurned Irishwoman's unwillingness to accept her former fiance's daughter. In *Presentation Parlour,* Kate O'Brien described how her Uncle Johnny, the handsome manager of the English and European branches of the family business, had once led the 'severe and ambitious' (108) Ann Liddy to believe he would marry her. When he rejected her, she married his eccentric eldest brother Mick, whose habit of collecting odds and ends appears in this novel's Uncle Corny, as does his inability to function effectively in the family horse-trading business. Even the rooms of the house, with their 'steel engravings in fine frames and little bright hunting pictures worked in silk' (46) replicate Shannon View, Uncle Mick's home. Uncle Johnny subsequently married a French ballerina or music-hall artist, and Kate O'Brien assumes that her aunt continued to love the man who rejected her. She continues their story in fiction by bringing the twenty-five-year-old actress Angèle Maury, whose father was Irish and mother a member of the *Comédie Française,* to the Drumaninch home of her aunt Hannah Kernahan.

In her responses to her family and to Ireland, and in their reactions to her, Angèle symbolises Kate O'Brien's feelings about the treatment of *The Land of Spices.* Angèle wishes to be accepted in Drumaninch, to live comfortably in a world that belongs to her past, only to discover that it holds no place for her. She finds the larger world outside, the Continent, finally more valuable, more worth fighting for than Drumaninch. France triumphs over Ireland in the battle for Angèle's identity. Although Angèle is a generation removed, she expresses the author's complex feelings towards the country that twice rejected her as an artist. In Angèle, as in Matt Costello, we recognise the author herself, the self-imposed emigrée, whose homeland repudiated her novels. As a representation of the creative personality, Angèle only minimally suggests an artist; she emerges simply as an attractive, dreamy young woman with theatrical ambitions who quotes lines from French drama and poetry. Nevertheless, her symbolic function is clear. Angèle reflects most specifically the Kate O'Brien who wrote *The Land of Spices,* the novel that most dramatically depicts the conflict bewteen Irish nationalist values and European culture.

After both her parents have died, Angèle impetuously visits Waterpark, her father's ancestral home in Ireland. The pilgrimage fuels the faint hope that she will understand why, as her father always said, she 'belonged to Drumaninch' (19). Thoroughly French, Angèle has no sense of her Irishness. Perhaps Waterpark can define it for her. But Angèle's arrival in Drumaninch immediately disquiets her and suggests that her father's world may be as dead to her as he is; she may not belong as much to his Drumaninch home as he had believed. 'In this most voluptuously beautiful and unusual land', she has been surprised and oppressed by 'an arrogance of austerity, contempt for personal feeling, coldness and perhaps fear of idiosyncrasy' (5). She intuits why her father — and surely, Kate O'Brien — left their land of birth; she empathises, in a 'pang of admiration the perfect rightness of living away from it, being its exile' (3). Yet, despite her uneasiness Angèle succmbs to the intense natural beauty of Ireland. Within a week of her arrival at Waterpark House, she falls in love, not only with its landscape, but with her first cousin Tom, who, of her three cousins living at Waterpark, is most identified with his home. Angèle decides to sacrifice her life in France and her theatrical aspirations for Tom, who has been named, we assume, for her father, his uncle, and the man his mother once loved.

Thus, Angèle expresses the desire to fuse her life with her father's by joining the Drumaninch family that her father had insisted was hers. Angèle's love for Tom reiterates the wish for a permanent place in her family that Kate O'Brien had portrayed in *Without My Cloak* and *The Ante-Room.* In her earliest novels, the characters, hostages to their families, tolerated, and, in some cases, enjoyed their captivity. The outcome of *The Last of Summer,* however, will differ greatly. No matter how primitive or powerful the pull, Angèle, like Mary Lavelle and Matt Costello, like those who have left the closed circle of Irish clan and country, cannot go back.

Tom and Angèle fall in love almost on sight, in a dazzling shock of emotions and senses. The flood of light in which they express their love is a tableau typical of Kate O'Brien's style: Tom and Angèle 'were standing curiously still . . . by the cleared table. The midnight light from sky and river fell all around them' (104). Angèle, reminding us of Mary Lavelle, tells Tom that their love will triumph over troubled reality:

There were pain and anxiety in her breast, but for once it seemed to her that she knew what she wanted. For how long, how cruelly, foolishly or rightly she had no way of guessing — her innocence denied her that, although her sense of orthodoxy would not spare her any of the outer barriers and dangers of what lay ahead . . . they seemed, for this moment at least, secondary things, though grave, and this other, this knowledge, was pure certainty. (105)

And Tom, believing that his life is less real than his love, that Angèle and the world that he has always known can somehow be conjoined, sounds very much like Juanito: 'I see that you're the reason for it all — and that you are a part of it for me now, and that I must give it all to you — and keep you here' (105).

But unlike Juanito, an intellectual and social critic, a full and fascinating character, Tom is almost a cipher. The reader knows no more of him than Angèle knows: he is handsome, close to his mother, and very much at one with the spirit of Waterpark House. Unlike his cosmopolitan brother Martin, who studies European history and has lived in and loves Paris, Tom seems to have little in common with Angèle except their lineage. Tom functions like Anna Hennessy and Richard Froude; more device than character, he embodies Angèle's wish to belong to her father's world. Tom is Angèle's tie to place and past.

Kate O'Brien suggests that we see Tom as the personification of Angèle's regressive desire for her father. Angèle recalls that her father always accompanied her mother on tour with the *Comèdie Française,* leaving Angèle in the care of their 'faithful, hard-faced *femme de menage*' (44). Repressing the pain of recurring unhappy childhood separations, Angèle minimises the effect of her father's lack of concern: 'Certainly her parents were much in love, and her father, quite rightly, preferred his wife to his little daughter. But a parent might, perhaps, in the exacting circumstances have considered the occasional sacrifice of his own preference — for his child's sake' (44). Angèle's tone and her aside, 'quite rightly', point to the oedipal drama she unwittingly attempts to conceal.

In marrying Tom, the representation of her father *before* he married Jeanne Maury, Angèle can satisfy her barely conscious desire to come first with her father — a wish we recognise as a pale mirror of Tom's intense relationship with his mother. Angèle's thoughts, moments after she and Tom have declared themselves to each other, further suggest the role he plays in her inner drama:

She felt foolish, happy, excited, indifferent to thought. Only her senses apprehended these minutes, this phase — accepting the river outside, and the room about her, the smell and hush of the living house . . . as if from memory, as if her father spoke of them . . . a whole moment, a proof of life. (123)

Kate O'Brien then immediately demonstrates Tom's regressive role:

Dans le trouble où je suis je ne puis rien pour moi, she said, stroking her shell and smiling — and she did not know whether she or, long ago, her mother said it. She said it again and again, listening to her mother and fitting the line's feet to the throb of the river. *Dans le trouble où je suis je ne puis rien pour moi.* The truth of that filled her senses and made her smile. (123-4)

Euphorically devoid of will, struggle, and choice, Angèle quotes Phèdre, a role her mother practised many times, but never played. Confusing her own voice with her mother's, she projects herself into Phèdre's incestuous passion. She does not yet recognise that her love for Tom will tie her to the past and subvert her autonomy. Ultimately, Angèle will also reject Tom, her father's replacement; maturity will vanquish incestuous love.

But in the larger social terms that are as significant to Kate O'Brien as unconscious longings, Angèle finds in Waterpark all that was lacking in her very different life in France. Continuity, stability, and tradition are as compelling to her as is Tom's attractiveness. Angèle's father, thoroughly bohemian in spirit, never worked; Jeanne Maury alone supported her family. As devoted as she was to the 'fixed traditions of French bourgeois and family life', her professional obligations required her absence from home many days and almost every evening and necessitated 'much changefulness of place and conditions'. As a result, her child had a 'fundamental sense of insecurity, which was always gallantly fought indeed, and never openly acknowledged'. Angèle grew up 'in a design of urban adjustments, made secure always because of her mother's trustworthiness, but retaining inescapably a character of *faute de mieux*' (43-4). Contrasting Angèle's France with Angèle's Ireland, Kate O'Brien conveys both the allure and the danger of Waterpark: 'Here in the house of her father's childhood she came on something very different . . . she sensed around her an assurance which possessed this family without its volition and depended on no living will but only on a sense of place and on the sunken years' (46). The instability of Angèle's childhood held none of the constancy of Waterpark, which Kate O'Brien describes in an atmosphere of foreboding; lacking in 'volition' and a 'living will', Waterpark seems deadly, the product of 'sunken years'. But it seems also to hold a promise of permanence and stability, and Tom personifies the promise: 'What could be better? she thought. What would I do if I had to marry someone — raw . . . with whom I had to go into a little empty house, a little bungalow or something . . . What would I make of him if he were just a chance acquaintance, by himself?' (172).

Angèle has only glimmerings that Tom represents repressed longings in herself, the father she has lost, the rootedness she never had. She cannot fathom why she grows fonder of Tom each day, but she senses that the explanation might lie in her childhood, 'far back in some long-fixed ideal she could never trace'. She associates her affection for Tom with a wish to satisfy her mother:

Certainly it touched and pleased her to realise that this marriage she was about to make would have pleased her mother. Establishment in country life, in a Catholic family of tradition and respectability; neither grossly rich nor very poor, with a husband who was young, good-looking, and good; and farewell, once and for all, to the insecurities, disappointments, and bitter triumphs of the theatre. (204)

Indeed, in marrying a Kernahan — a Tom, at that — Angèle is doing what her mother had done, but with a very obvious difference: Angèle's father had lived in France, become French legally and culturally, and accepted the exile's rootless existence. Angèle would give it all up. She knows that Angèle Kernahan would be very different from Angèle Maury, but she does not yet understand the many implications: 'She would cease to be an actress, now. And she would cease to be French. Everything she knew and had been would go, and she would begin all over again. Like a pioneer, like an exile' (128). She would live her father's life in reverse; without recognising the ominous suggestiveness of her thoughts, Angèle imagines that she 'would live in this lonely, quiet place, with a handful of odd and ageing people; in love with Tom. She would have Tom's children, and become what her father had refused to be, a Kernahan of Waterpark House' (128).

Responding to Tom with her 'heart and senses', Angèle acknowledges that 'each actual moment *just* fail[s] to become real' (165), but the lovers think their emotions will endure. It is the other characters and the narrator who insist that such love is a short-lived illusion. Tom's brother Martin, the novel's realist — somewhat suspect for he, too, is infatuated with Angèle — expresses Kate O'Brien's truth most blatantly. To Angèle's declaration of love for Tom, he responds, 'Oh rot! Romantic drivel! We are what we are born and bred and work in — not what we feel in our senses all of a sudden one summer night' (198). Tom is bound by the codes of Waterpark, and Angèle by those of Paris. The lovers fantasise merging the codes; Martin insists they cannot. Tom's sister Jo, who lacks Martin's personal stake in the relationship, also points out the folly of their feelings. Jo insists that the 'innocence and purity of [Angèle's] eyes, the intelligence of her high wide brow, and the whole exaggerated grace of her' are 'angelic . . . and the nature of a dream'. It is no wonder, she thinks, that Tom, 'the innocent dreamer', should 'come home to full desire in such a myth' (164).

But it is the omniscient narrator, speaking for the author, who comments most poignantly on the inherent weakness of romantic love. As soon as Angèle admits that she loves Tom 'enough' to marry him, to give up all that she is and has been, the narrator adds:

She did not realise yet how very operative and significant was the adverb 'enough' with which she supported her new affirmation ... She did not know that this was almost never true, and that it was not manifest to many lovers even within the very pleasure of the first embrace. Love can survive, a little or a long time, this lesson of its insufficiency — because it must, because self-love and self-respect insist; because pleasure is strong and compromise is an understood necessity, and because lovers learn to understand love cynically and yet value it. (122)

Again, Kate O'Brien reminds us that love is never strong enough to overcome its inevitable impediments.

But objections to Angèle and Tom's union are not based merely on the author's cynicism towards romantic love. Tom is inexorably tied to his mother, memories of his childhood, and domestic security. He has enjoyed with his mother what Angèle sought and believes she has found in her father's home. More than his brother and sister, Tom has yielded to, and built his life upon, his youth. Of the three, he most 'remembered childhood with devotion, and was constantly hurt and made anxious by the breaches which the grown-up years made and made again in a unit which once had been impregnable' (75). And, in his childlike innocence, Tom believes that he need not change his life for Angèle, that she can simply be absorbed into the fabric of life at Waterpark. He does not perceive how his love will affect his mother, even though he has remained her 'perfect' (231) son, replacing all that she lost when the elder Tom spurned her. Hannah gives him all the love she never gave his father. He is the passion in her life that Angèle's father had been, and Hannah is determined never again to suffer its loss.

Hannah not only prefers Tom to her other children; she worships him 'inordinately' (113). But her love is self-centred and selfish; for thirteen years, Tom has had to fill his father's shoes and satisfy Hannah's emotional greed. While his life has not always been easy, Tom has taken great, perhaps excessive, pleasure in assuring his mother of her place:

He had worked very hard and had learnt how to carry large anxieties; but in return he lived in the place he loved best on earth, and he had not only his mother's love but also her counsels and good sense perpetually at his disposal — with her smile and prettiness thrown in as added bounty of which he never tired. Always she pleased his eyes as no other woman did; always, if she wished to, she could make him laugh. It seemed a good life to him — worthwhile and lucky and founded on traditions and duties that he understood. (76-7)

In addition, Tom hears from all around him — priests, nuns, family friends — that his mother is 'wonderful, a saint, a credit to her sex, that she had suffered as few are called upon to suffer, and that he must . . . always bear [it] in mind' (76). He never needs reminding. From his earliest years he saw his mother as the personification of beauty and goodness, and he took charge of her home 'with an immense and proud delight' (76). When Martin and Jo left to pursue their studies at university and in Europe, Tom lived at Waterpark, raising horses and cattle, and with Hannah, salvaged their home from the fiscal disarray in which his father had left it. Hannah is the core of his existence, and Tom eschews whatever excludes his mother or removes her 'from first place in his life' (125). He 'never went to his room, never did anything on his evening return to the house, before he came to the drawing room to find mother and tell her about the day' (154).

Controlling her environment with steely certainty, Hannah feeds, and feeds on, the myth that it was she who rejected Tom Kernahan. She relishes the images others have of her:

A woman in a million. The greatest beauty of her day in Mellick, with the three Kernahan brothers — and not they alone! — at each other's throats about her. And now look at her — the best of Catholic mothers, unselfish and devoted, a most charitable and perfect lady, a widow who had suffered many's the dark trial all through her married life, and had had to keep her beautiful home together and bring up her children single-handed — an example to us all. (113)

Her friends and all her children subscribe to the myth, including Martin and Jo who know that Tom is her favourite. Even as they see flashes of Hannah's hypocrisy, Martin and Jo help to maintain her pristine public image. Angèle notes Jo's 'touching' anxiety to keep her mother's 'screens in position, and to dismiss an offensiveness which must not be admitted to exist' (26). But most important to Hannah is that Tom continue to adore her. Unconsciously, Tom sacrifices a normal life and natural desires on the altar of filial devotion. He is blind to the bitterness and irony that thread through this description of his life:

There were shames and needs which a mother could not possibly be expected to imagine; there were lonelinesses which her understanding would, thank Heaven, never compass, and sins of which she would never hear hint or rumour . . . they were the private problem of any man, and the Church was there, after all, to help him solve it. It might sometimes seem as if early manhood was easier, more naturally controlled, in those who were more free than he, who were not so tenderly loved by so sensitive and devoted a parent . . . But . . . living with goodness made a man value it; made him contemptuous of his own inclination to evil. (77)

Even as he loses Angèle to his mother's manipulation, Tom see Hannah only as 'perfect', an 'angel' (158), ultimately his only angel. He is a willing Hippolyte to her Phèdre.

If Jeanne Maury was never able to play her favourite role, Hannah, the novel's one truly superb actress, plays it all too well. Recurrent allusions to Racine's drama reinforce the novel's troubled time-warp, its inter-generational confusion. Angèle, too, imagines herself as Phèdre whenever she recalls her mother's rehearsing the line in which Phèdre reveals her forbidden love for her step-son: *'Athènes me montra mon superbe ennemi'*. Hannah, at Drumaninch, is Angèle's 'superbe ennemi'.

But Kate O'Brien relies not only on Hannah to convey the malignancy of a mother's unremitting involvement with her son. Just as she drew on Dr Curran in *The Ante-Room*, Kate O'Brien draws on the authority of a man of science and reason to reinforce her condemnation of Hannah. Dr O'Byrne, the family doctor, tries to persuade Hannah to relinquish her hold so that Tom might be free to marry his daughter, who grew up with Tom and loves him. Dr O'Byrne has never encountered 'as selfish a case of mother love' (137). And when he suggests to Hannah that she has kept Tom from normal expressions of his masculinity, Hannah warns the doctor about intruding on the sanctity of a mother's relationship with her son; 'I *have* heard', she says, 'of the messes some interferers try to make nowadays of simple natural things' (141). But what is natural to Hannah is highly unnatural to Dr O'Byrne, who wishes his daughter happily married. He insists that it is not only the modern, post-Freudian world that has labeled 'unhealthy' such liaisons as Hannah and Tom's; such 'messes' are 'older than Sophocles . . . as old as Egypt, or Genesis; and none the healthier for having temples built above them' (141). Dr O'Byrne chastises Hannah, 'What's the matter with you? . . . Don't you face life at all here in your watch tower? Don't you know that a man *must* have the natural gratifications that no maternal piety can blind him to?' (147-8). The other characters also detect the flaw. Martin, for example, says, 'Tom will be weaned some day — and then he'll want a wife' (37).

The Last of Summer takes place between Tuesday 22 August and Sunday 3 September 1939. Savagery descends, both between Angèle and Hannah and between Germany and Poland, and incites France and Britain to declare war. Kate O'Brien uses her characters to make a political point. The withdrawal from military action in Europe underscores the national self-absorption that flourished in Ireland after the establishment of the Free State. The attitudes that Kate O'Brien once portrayed as characteristic of her own class, she now says are typical of the nation, in general. In *The Last of Summer,* more stridently than elsewhere in her novels, the personal, the familial and the political all point to the same structures of character and belief governing Irish life. Personal and political mirror each other; Hannah and Tom together are the familial form of Ireland's isolationism, and Angèle, who confronts them, is Europe in turmoil. But it is primarily Hannah Kernahan, in her absorption with Tom, home and Ireland, who personifies the country's invidious detachment.

Hannah is indifferent 'to everything and everyone not directly or very nearly connected with herself'. She desires only what she can 'own, rule, absorb'. She lives in 'a passion of privacy, requiring only for her happiness the fantasy she . . . made of herself, and the belief of her modest entourage in that fantasy — above all, the belief in it of her son Tom, who was both its source and its proof' (145). Nothing else matters, and nothing can intrude on Hannah's myth. She never leaves Waterpark; everyone — clergy, family member, friend — comes to her. 'Whatever concerns Waterpark constitutes her life' (26), and in her voluntary insularity, Hannah is Kate O'Brien's Ireland.

Hannah's myopia, in fact, distorts her view of Ireland's position regarding Europe directly. As she denies life outside Waterpark, she denies life outside Eire. She is the novel's vehement — though not its only — spokesman for the legitimacy of Ireland's isolation and neutrality. Hannah is quite conscious that her attitudes towards the war are just an extension of her attitudes towards Tom and Waterpark. Refuting the inevitability of the conflagration, she is cutting and contemptible, even if her remarks are meant to justify her wish to keep her world safe. Her complacency is frightening. When Martin, who with Jo, is acutely involved in the events abroad, warns of the 'trouble going on in Danzig', Hannah's denial, 'Danzig's a long way from Drumaninch, my son' (179), has no equal even among the smuggest of Kate O'Brien's characters. But the certainty with which she speaks momentarily convinces even Martin.

As war appears inevitable, Hannah becomes all the more tenacious. '*We're* not having it, Martin. It's nothing whatever to do with us. A plague on both their houses' (193). To rationalise her position, she minimises the imminent encounter. She maintains that England is making 'a pretext out of a mere frontier dispute between Germany and Poland' (194). Martin laughs 'outright', but his ridicule has little effect. Even when Germany invades Poland and occupies Danzig, ensuring the entrance of France and England in the war, Hannah remains shockingly detached. And each time she speaks of it, the other characters, particularly Martin, articulate Kate O'Brien's contempt. Hannah tries to rally the mood of the young people, who are 'white faced' at the news of the invasion, asking, 'Why all this fuss about *Poland?*' Martin, enraged, answers, 'Great Christ Almighty! For the last and lucky time, I tell you, Mother — it *isn't* a fuss about Poland'. Hannah inevitably responds, 'But my darling boy it is' (217).

Were Hannah the only character to find comfort in Ireland's isolationism, the country's neutrality would appear less perilous, merely an expression of Hannah's psychopathology, but Angèle reflects the dangerous power of that allure:

Angèle had forgotten for hours that now seemed countless that there was such a thing as the nine o'clock news, with a whole world waiting on it in fear. She wondered if the others had forgotten . . . She felt the peace of the moment as sharply as if she knew an alarm bell was about to clang against it instantly. (95)

Even Dr O'Byrne, who, in a sense, represents Irish reason and functions as a foil to Hannah, is comforted by Ireland's stance. When Martin asks if he has heard 'any news' about the war, the doctor, as removed as Hannah, answers, 'Something about incidents on the Polish frontier, I think . . . but to tell you the truth I dozed a bit while they were crooning it out at me' (102). Like Hannah, Dr O'Byrne and most Irish people sleep the forgetful sleep of Tir-na-nogue and support the neutrality that Kate O'Brien condemns.

Despite his intense awareness of the war, Martin, when he first returned to Ireland from Europe, was also seduced by Ireland's removal from the problems abroad. Even he succumbed to the lotus land. He appreciated Drumaninch's denial of contemporary Europe:

It was fine to be simply unable to get hold of a *Corriere della Sera* or a *Berliner Tageblatt* or a *Journal des Débats,* and to know that even if one did exert oneself to buy a *Times* or a *Manchester Guardian,* it would be a day old, quite useless. So he hardly glanced at the *Daily Express,* Irish edition, though sometimes, in sheer wonder, he read de Valera's official newspaper, *The Irish Press.* (187)

But the opiate wears off as Martin and his sister Jo signal Hannah's insularity and narcissism. An Irishman who sees beyond his country's borders and who is concerned with Europe's past and present, Martin cannot remain passive or 'neutral' in the face of potential destruction. 'His nerves' tell him that war is 'very near now' (187), and he grows restless, listens more to the news, and scans any newspapers he can find. When tensions in Europe appear hopelessly frayed, Martin leaves Ireland to fight in the French Army. He is willing to sacrifice his life, not for maternal love, but for the human community. He cannot withdraw; he is too much a part of the world beyond Eire.

Jo, too, is occupied with the war and speaks as the novel's moral voice. The outbreak of violence confirms her decision to become a nun. She will join the *Couvent de la Sainte Famille* not in retreat, but, updating and revising the alternative of the religious life, she will go to Europe, to do 'something Christian . . . for refugees or children or in air raids' (208). She acknowledges the 'political' rightness of Ireland's position, but insists:

> Eire will be neutral, which is only the clearest common sense, politically. But that's beside the point. Little patches of immunity like ours are going to be small consolation for what's coming. Being neutral will be precious little help to the imagination, I should think. (81)

As Dr O'Byrne astutely recognises, 'It seems we'll be lonely here in our neutrality!' (242).

The closed world Angèle enters in the novel offers small welcome and little detachment. Hannah proves too formidable an opponent. Lonely for France and frightened by the prospect of losing all she has known and loved to the devastation of war, Angèle is not willing to stay and fight for Tom. She concedes defeat to Hannah and sets out for France. The world she has been 'born and bred and worked in' (198), the world of the Rue d'Estrées, of theatre dressing rooms and movie studios, with all the faults and disappointments of childhood, is finally more important than her love for Tom. Leaving Drumaninch, Angèle stands 'as if in the centre of a dream . . . In four hours these ten days of fantasy would have slid into the formal shapes of memory, and she would be on her way to war' (241).

Angèle awakens to face the horror ahead. By fleeing to France, to the world of her mother and her youth, she leaves childhood and its dreams behind. Her commitment is to a past different from Tom's; it is a commitment to the larger world of engagement, to struggles and conflicts between nations, to those who see the defence of Europe as their moral obligation. Despite its personal significance, Angèle's return to France is not regressive. In the farewell conversation between Jo and Angèle, Kate O'Brien suggests that Angèle's decision to return must not be equated with Tom's ties to his mother. Jo jokes that both Angèle and Tom 'have the Oedipus Complex' (238), not referring to Angèle's curiosity about her late father but using the Freudian term erroneously to speak of Angèle's love for her mother. More to the point, in leaving Tom, Angèle is resolving her 'Oedipus Complex'. At the book's conclusion, Angèle no longer repeats the lines from *Phèdre* that Waterpark evoked. Instead, the last lines of French she recites fulfil Martin's request that she 'say something in French . . . say the very first line of French verse that comes into [her] head' (216). She speaks not from her mother's beloved Racine, but from Baudelaire's *Recueillement:* '*Sois sage, ô ma Douleur, et tiens-toi plus tranquille*'. Exercising compassion and the imagination that Kate O'Brien insists the 'neutral'

Irish lack, Angèle makes the difficult choice to face misery, disaster, and death.

If Angèle's experience in Ireland is Kate O'Brien's dramatisation of the nation's treatment of *The Land of Spices,* Jo and, particularly, Martin represent the author's solution and response to it. Rejected again by her homeland, Kate O'Brien rejects it for Europe. Perhaps her yearning for Ireland, in fiction if not in fact, was her 'Oedipus Complex'. Like Martin, she understands the inevitable sadness in family life, knows a 'warm illusion' must 'split up and leave its units to cool off as they can' (216).

If *The Land of Spices* was a return to childhood, *The Last of Summer* is, even at the risk of personal destruction, a turning towards adulthood and independence, away from Ireland. Kate O'Brien condemns the self-protecting, self-righteous culture that, lacking empathy, denies participation in the world and, lacking imagination, censors its artists.

Eight

That Lady

As *The Last of Summer* ended, Kate O'Brien's heroine repudiated Ireland and returned to the Continent, to a world that seemed, even at war, more worth fighting for than the Irish backwater upon which she had stumbled. In *That Lady*,[1] her next novel, published in 1946, the author again turns her back on Ireland as her setting in favour of sixteenth-century Spain and portrays more starkly than ever the central conflict of her writings — the struggle between personal freedom and social compliance. In *The Last of Summer* and *Mary Lavelle,* Kate O'Brien symbolically connected the psychological conflicts of her characters with their political realities, suggesting larger social issues in their personal dramas. In *That Lady,* however, there was no need to create symbolic ties between the public and the private because, in the four-hundred-year-old incident that occurred in the court of Philip II and in which Ana de Mendoza, the Princess of Eboli, gained notoriety, these spheres were already fused and ready for the author's scrutiny and application.

Of all the countries in Europe, Spain had always beckoned most strongly to Kate O'Brien. In *Mary Lavelle* she suggested the reason: individualism thrived there amid reverence for the common good. The social pressures that thwarted Mary's personal desire suggested the political oppression that was to destroy Spain under Franco's rule. The central issues in *Mary Lavelle* become more urgent in *That Lady* as Kate O'Brien brings to life a scandalised member of Philip's court. In one of her most self-revealing strokes of irony, Kate O'Brien arranges for an intensely private person to fall from grace as all of Europe watches. Ana de Mendoza becomes Kate O'Brien's most compelling portrait of the individualist, and, of all her heroines, the one who speaks loudest and most passionately for the author's commitment to self-expression. 'That lady' is her idealisation of the woman who lives according to her beliefs, who will sacrifice prestige, power, and liberty, defending her right to effect her 'life in action' (118). Writing as the author of two books banned in Ireland, Kate O'Brien retaliates through Ana. Ana's vengeance proves that if the search for the self leads to public catastrophe, it can also lead to private triumph.

The incident on which *That Lady* is based is one of the most controversial and enigmatic events in the reign of Philip II: the murder, in 1578, of his secretary Juan de Escovedo. In *Antonio Pérez,* a study of one of Philip's secretaries of state, Gregorio Marañón summarises the various historical re-creations of the episode. He tells us that after the Princess of Eboli, one of the most powerful women in Spain, was widowed, she became Pérez's mistress. Another of the king's secretaries, Juan de Escovedo, 'surprised Doña Ana and Antonio enacting scenes of scandalous intimacy'.[2] When the outraged Escovedo threatened to report them, the adulterers conspired to be rid of him. According to Marañón, in the most commonly accepted, highly sensationalised version, the princess urged Antonio to convince the already-suspicious king that Secretary Escovedo was engaged in treachery. Philip ordered Escovedo executed without trial and resisted trying the lovers when he learned of their deceit, lest he incriminate himself. Lurid and unfounded details added over time to this basic narrative variously suggest that even before the Prince of Eboli died, the princess had been Philip's mistress and that the prince condoned the affair to assure his standing with Philip. In some renderings, Antonio is said to have acted as a go-between to forward his own political position (84). All accounts of the incident confirm that one year after the murder, Philip arrested Ana and Antonio without charges, in the name of their own safety. The princess was jailed for fourteen years until her death at fifty-two, deprived of the control of her estates and the guardianship of her children. Antonio was imprisoned and, nearly eleven years later, put to the rack, when he implicated the king in the Escovedo killing. So doing, he escaped to France and lived his final years in exile.

That Lady begins with the author's puzzling disclaimer of historical fidelity:

What follows is not a historical novel. It is an invention arising from reflection on the curious external story of Ana de Mendoza and Philip II of Spain. Historians cannot explain the episode, and the attempt is not made in a work of fiction. All the personages in this book lived, and I have retained the historical outline of events in which they played a part; but everything which they say or write in my pages is invented, and — naturally — so are their thoughts and emotions. And in order to retain unity of invention I have refrained from grafting into my fiction any part of their recorded letters or observations. (xiv)

The foreword is disconcerting in its inaccuracy, for *That Lady* is most assuredly a historical novel, offering a plausible, if romantic, explanation for its 'curious external story'. *That Lady* fits our common assumptions about the historical novel so well, its interpretation of the episode seems so authentic and credible, that one must ask why Kate O'Brien protests.

Perhaps the answer lies in the degree to which she personalises her historical characters and their actions. Her Ana, for example, is blameless and ignorant of Escovedo's murder until after it happens, and guilty only of her love for Antonio and her wish to express it. She becomes Kate O'Brien's ideal of a woman who wishes to be autonomous and independent. A martyr in the quest for a private life, thirty-six-year-old Ana has had time to frame her moral outlook and to learn to resist external pressure, even the demands of absolute monarchy. She moves with the self-confidence and certainty of vision that comes only with a depth of experience.

Neither a nun nor a dutiful daughter relegated to her ancestral home, Ana is Kate O'Brien's most mature and most public heroine, the *only* female to have lived fully. She is worldly enough to decide her actions and obligations for herself. A wife, mother, widow, and mistress, Ana enables the author to examine from many vantage points the meaning and consequences of the search for personal freedom in the face of the most stringent, most explicit public mandates. Perhaps Kate O'Brien's disclaimer arises from her identification with her heroine. Did the author believe that in weaving her own struggles for nonconformity and self-sufficiency into Ana's relationships with Philip and his minister Antonio Pérez, she had failed the demands of historicity and betrayed the genre?

Furthermore, Kate O'Brien may have read into the historical Ana's story and setting not merely personal parallels, but also compelling analogues to contemporary Europe. There, absolute power prevailed to the greatest extent history has yet known, and individual rights were even more in jeopardy than in the time of Philip II. With an eye towards the violent upheavals that had just ravaged the European continent, Kate O'Brien presents the Escovedo assassination, its causes and effects, within the context of Spain's weakening position in Europe and Philip's anxiety over the erosion of his empire. Its enormous holdings in America notwithstanding, Spain is bankrupt, and all of Europe knows it. The Netherlands are in disarray; France poses an inevitable Protestant menace to Spanish hegemony; England must be watched and appeased; Venice is a questionable ally, and the Turks are restive. Philip's frantic efforts to keep his empire intact must have seemed to Kate O'Brien the prototype of Hitler's madness; in Philip's despotism she surely saw an ancestor of the oppression raging in Europe that denied independence to the individual and the right of every man to have his say — literally, to have his day in court. As Lorna Reynolds has suggested, with the story of Ana de Mendoza, Kate O'Brien pays tribute to the heroes of World War II who fought and died defending political freedom against tyranny.[3]

In discarding her dispassion, the author, like her heroine, denies the tyranny of circumstance. Acknowledging subjectivity as a part of all historical novels — even if Kate O'Brien cannot — the reader accepts the remarkable Ana de Mendoza as a projection of Kate O'Brien. The disparities between the legend and *That Lady* illustrate the extent to which Kate O'Brien has made the story her own. Beauty, prominence, power, and strength of will are all common to the princess's many historical portraits. Most accounts present her as 'a haughty, passionate termagant, who . . . since her husband's death had given a great deal of trouble to the king, by her erratic and impracticable conduct'.⁴ In one she is 'indiscreet, ambitious, capricious, and volatile';⁵ in another she is 'ill-tempered', 'domineering', and given to 'feudal' imperiousness. Living 'a life of scandalous luxury', she is said to have nearly ruined her estates through 'disorderliness'. Her family calls her 'mad'.⁶

Kate O'Brien is far kinder. In *That Lady,* Ana is an austere aristocrat, an ascetic who calms all in her presence, speaks directly and with dignity, and takes pride in the productivity and orderliness of her estates. She is honourable, loyal, and loving — but only to those, even among her children, who merit her love by the exacting standards she applies first to herself. She is her own highest authority. In contrast to the Ana of legend, she enters prison stoically and refuses to feign contrition to relieve her suffering. Kate O'Brien's revision of Ana's character into an unyielding individual dramatises the theme central to all her works: the conflict between personal independence and public law, whether moral, social, or political.

The Antonio Pérez of history is a fascinating figure. He came into power as a young man, ingratiating himself with Philip, until he became the king's highest ranking secretary. A commoner with lordly inclinations, Antonio was arrogant, extravagant, and notoriously promiscuous, yet a man of unusual charm who exercised unprecedented influence on the king's foreign policy. He abused his power, however, selling public offices for vast sums and robbing the royal treasury. Historians suggest that Antonio, together with the Princess of Eboli, was engaged in treason in the Netherlands and Portugal.⁸ One of Philip's biographers describes Antonio as 'a liar, a forger, a slanderer, a murderer, a thorough-going scoundrel'.⁹

Although, in *That Lady,* Kate O'Brien retains history's materialistic dandy and politically powerful womaniser, she crafts a far more benign and sympathetic Antonio — one worthy of her Ana — who serves the king fairly and indefatigably. His loyalty to Philip is unquestionable; at the king's order he murders Escovedo for his treachery in the Netherlands. Ana knows Antonio to be loving, attentive, and understanding. Kate O'Brien's recasting, however, robs him of much of his colour. He is the least compelling of the novel's central characters and, like Richard Froude, is an example of her ineffective male portraits. In her failure to bring Antonio to life, Kate O'Brien again reveals her disbelief in romantic love between men and women. A convenient cause for the friction between Ana and Philip, Antonio becomes more an instrument of plot than a fully realised protagonist.

Kate O'Brien's Philip is closer to the psychological portraits his biographers have assembled.[10] Overworked, harried, and besieged with anxieties for his state and his soul, he is overwhelming in his power, but balances attentiveness to statecraft with a passion for nature, art, and music. A loving husband and father, he is merciless to those he perceives as his enemies. He is fanatically vigilant over the cause of Catholicism in Spain, Europe, and the New World. One aspect of Kate O'Brien's treatment of Philip, however, is crucial to the novel and distinguishes him from his historical model: his passionate obsession for Ana. In Kate O'Brien's portrait, Philip's love is constant and dominant — the primary determinant in his decisions and actions. Yet, like earlier scholars with a 'respect for the truth',[11] Kate O'Brien denies that Philip and Ana have been lovers. Philip rightly believes that Ana would have been his mistress had he ever wished it, but his friendship and respect for her husband, and his need, like Kate O'Brien's, to idealise Ana prevent him from consummating their love. Theirs is a far more subtle relationship. Philip is thoroughly possessive. He 'reserved' (23) Ana for her husband, and he believes that, in every sphere of her life, she is still his to command. Philip makes no distinction between the loyalty she owes him as his subject and her privacy as an individual. She is simply his. That another man has physically possessed Ana drives him mad with jealousy. His passion is the most vicious version of the possessive love that Kate O'Brien presented with such ambivalence in *Without My Cloak,* and with such antipathy in *The Last of Summer.* She transforms Philip II into her most devastating symbol of the love that kills.

Lorna Reynolds[12] has suggested that the most likely sources for Kate O'Brien's portrait of Ana de Mendoza are St Teresa's *Letters* and *Foundations.* Kate O'Brien speaks of both with great delight[13] in her study of the saint written in 1951, five years after *That Lady.* In the *Foundations,* St Teresa tactfully recounted her efforts to establish a monastery at Pastrana under the patronage of the Prince and Princess of Eboli and described the princess's attempt to join the Carmelites after her husband's death. To serve the political needs of her order, the saint described the princess with a restraint that belied her experience as well as records of the event.[14] History tells us that the princess made overweening and inappropriate demands on the saint, denounced her *Life* to the Inquisition as heresy (the Inquisition delivered a favourable judgment that Kate O'Brien might well have wished for her own novels), and, when she left the monastery, withheld the alms she and her husband had promised the Carmelites. Poverty ultimately forced the order to leave Pastrana.

To serve her needs, Kate O'Brien treats Ana's behaviour even more delicately than did St Teresa and creates a richer and more sympathetic psychological portrait. She depicts the episode the saint described — the princess's intemperate entrance into the Carmelites and failure to unite her life with the saint's — as that of a woman trying, however unconventionally, to find herself. As a wife, Ana had submitted to her husband's 'quiet, insistent domination'; as a widow, she felt 'a sense of total incompetence, of being a cripple' (117) and her years of marital subjugation, a waste. Her wish to enter the convent grows from an insistent need for self-discovery. As Ana lurches towards the independence that marriage had denied, the reader sees her as merely misguided and ill-fated: 'Had she ever been able — indulged great lady from birth — to accept the rules of a religious house, this was not the time, when she was ill, deranged, and derangedly set on doing what was unnatural' (117). This is no portrait of a selfish, wilful princess, but rather a solicitous study of a bereaved woman who has erred gracelessly in her search for individuality.

Once before, Ana had attempted to define herself and had suffered disfigurement. According to Kate O'Brien, she lost an eye as a 'spoiled and arrogant' adolescent, defending the honour of Castile. (According to legend, the blinding occurred during 'rapier play with some page or gentleman'.)[15] 'Her soldierly sacrifice' (86) becomes a touchstone for Ana. Whenever she is about to defy public or social expectations, she presses the black silk patch that covers the empty socket of her eye. Each touch foreshadows further maiming for the sake of freedom and individuality. The blinding of her eye and her failure to become a nun, are both personal symbols,

sharp sentries over her general, surprised sense of never having managed to be herself throughout her singularly successful life. Both, she half-guessed, were answerable for the hour, the unforeseen moment in which, visited by a physical desire so precise as to be cold and shocking, she had made herself mistress of Antonio Pérez. (118)

Kate O'Brien uses these dramatic historical incidents as keys to understanding Ana's relationships with Antonio and Philip II. In taking a lover and continually defying Philip, Ana perpetuates a personal odyssey that in its initial steps had maimed and embarrassed her. Kate O'Brien goes beyond merely suggesting that the measures undertaken in behalf of self-definition inevitably hurt and humiliate. In *That Lady* she posits that such trials mould and define the self. Ana knows that her past actions foretell a painful outcome to her affair with Antonio and her defiance of Philip, that before the Church and society committing adultery is as disfiguring as the loss of an eye. But she is powerless to predict how dearly she will have to pay for her challenge to convention. Almost from the beginning of her search 'to feel somehow persuaded about herself' (188), Ana has known that 'private life . . . must surely be about something more than the commonplace of any street or bed. There still must be a reason . . . for being oneself, and this is not it. Suffering perhaps, or conflict or faith or an argument or a test of some kind' (88). A test indeed. Ana will discover, as Matt Costello did in *Pray for the Wanderer,* that to be oneself is, at the very least, to be outcast.

The ultimate test of selfhood begins for Kate O'Brien's Ana when Juan de Escovedo finds her in bed with Antonio. As Escovedo rages at the sinful lovers, Ana envisions herself 'in hell' (122); her 'soul has no place in [Antonio's] arms' (180). Her third attempt at individuation will deform her still further, perhaps for all eternity. The wound she incurred as an adolescent augurs the wound she chooses as an adult:

I am marked for the grotesque, she told herself, as she had before, in the relentless night. And, alone, she would take off her black diamond patch. She would stare then in the mirror at her hungry, long face, so halved and split into blankness, and at the closed and dark-stained empty socket of her eye. And she would think of . . . the cold beastliness of calculated love-pleasure, and the absurdity of sexual delight. And she would pace her room and long for the cocks to crow in daylight. (129)

But Escovedo's murder has endangered the lovers, particularly Antonio, politically as well as spiritually. Ana lays aside concern for her soul's salvation and sets a course in which Antonio's practical needs supersede her spiritual ones:

When all was well with him I took with both hands all I wanted, and cared very little about my soul or his. Now, now when the world I enjoy and know so well the world he works so hard for is gathering up excuses to destroy him — is now my time to harass him with convent metaphysics, and the entirely private, small question of my soul?

'Absurd, preposterous' . . .

Is my poor scruple greater than what I give this man and take from him? Am I to set my little private sense of sin above his claim on me and his unhappiness? (181-2)

And Ana redefines her love. No longer is it 'simply physical passion, calculated love-pleasure and . . . sexual delight'; her love is 'henceforward what traditionally she understood it to be — a Christian passion' (190). Reconciling the demands of adulterous love with Christianity, as, in *The Land of Spices,* Mère Marie-Hélène reconciled her father's homosexuality, Ana experiences physical pleasure wedded to kindness and charity. From then on,

> she was Antonio's lover on new and shifting terms — because of this and because of that, because he needed her, because there were moods when she couldn't do without him, because friends were failing him, because she loved him — for every stormy reason of a heart that has grown truly warm towards another; but not any longer now because she was simply in love. (190-91)

Ana's interpretation of Christian doctrine runs counter to every orthodoxy. She cannot repent, nor can she deny the claims of Antonio's love: 'This is not the time for private piety. Heaven must make what it likes of my confusion. That is a risk I have the right to take' (195). She insists that her first obligation is to her lover.

In what we recognise as another irony — and mode of thought — typical of Kate O'Brien's heroines, Ana chooses the conventionally immoral course, insisting that it is, for her, the only truly moral one. Many of Kate O'Brien's heroines have insisted on their own moral definitions, on making their own choices against the teachings of their Church and their culture. But Ana's choice entails the greatest personal cost, her physical freedom. She will lose all but her belief in her own rectitude.

Kate O'Brien asks that we applaud Ana's preference for love over dogma. When Ana acknowledges that she has sinned for the man she loves, even Cardinal Quiroga, Archbishop of Toledo, approves her courage and principle: 'God forgive me! I admire you a little' (196). But Ana's decision to redirect her private life from spiritually selfish to selflessly Christian demands that her personal affairs be made public and political. Kate O'Brien knew well that public demands in the private domain often become intensely political. Her Ana realises that, for safety and sanctity, she, too, must move into the public arena. Ana will demonstrate to all observers the indisputability of Antonio's innocence and forswear any accountability for Escovedo's death. To save Antonio, she will sacrifice the privacy she craves by admitting to their adultery, but she will also make clear that their love affair has no bearing on the murder. Deliberately fuelling the gossip she has always generated, Ana is particularly bold in her public stand against Philip: 'why on earth should he *not* hear [of the affair]? If it annoys him, I shall be flattered, and touched. But beyond the prick to his already half-dead vanity, it isn't his affair — our being lovers' (171). Spain is 'a country of free people', she reasons, and 'if it actually came to victimisation of Antonio because of Philip's conceit, she would enjoy asking the king how he dared intrude himself thus upon another's privacy?' (179). Ana continually denies King Philip's right to control her, discounting any

man's lordship over her days or her actions . . . Philip might enter her drawing-room when he chose, and like or not whom he found there, as he chose. As to her right to do as she pleased in her own house she no more regarded Philip's judgment than that of the youngest washer-up in her kitchen. (97)

At a time when the Divine Right of Kings is the accepted doctrine, Ana's position is daringly modern. She moves the novel into the twentieth century, to the war years in Europe, when individual rights and the democratic process are at even greater risk than in Philip's day. More strongly than Matt Costello, she speaks to the immorality of public intervention in private affairs. She maintains the political stance of the individual opposed to control by monarch or state: 'Our private lives don't belong to the king' (142). Ana rues Philip's deafness to the *vox populi;* her hope is that he will respect her demand that the Escovedo case be brought to trial, the matter handed over to the people of Castile. In Kate O'Brien's portrait, Ana becomes a spokeswoman for independence, for the safeguarding of private boundaries, and for the preservation of legal rights.

Philip's reluctance to bring Antonio to court, his silence, and his unwillingness ever to speak her name (she is only 'that lady') puzzle Ana. Protected by his Divine Right, he has little to lose. Christian in her love, Ana cannot impute a malignant motive to the man from which she has always felt warmth and affection: 'these were signs of something other beside hardening of his heart. That Lady. She knew that it was not for nothing, not cheaply or cruelly that she became That Lady on Philip's lips' (222). Having created an Ana staunchly loyal to the goodness Philip has always shown her, Kate O'Brien can also paint a psychological portrait of the monarch who, for so many centuries, evoked radically different views, according to the religious or political affiliations of his historians. Ana, to whom he has always appeared 'reasonable, considerate, gentle, faithful . . . a man who could not resist any direct appeal of poverty or of little children, or of the holy, or the mad, or the sick' (233), views Philip's current behaviour as simply incomprehensible. She cannot accept a man who truly believes that he, king or not, can dictate her personal conduct. Why his 'haggling'; why his turning against her without cause? 'She outraged no claim of his in loving another man, and her private life was her own' (233).

After months of silence, Philip finally speaks to Ana, and he is overwhelmed. He cannot bear that she, who had been his in fantasy,

is the mistress of one of his subjects. Ana adroitly counters his
accusations of adulterous disgrace and disloyalty and his threat to
command her to apologise publicly:

You know that I have always been . . . childishly and fanatically your subject . . .
You know that in everything of me that your office commands I am absolutely
yours. But if you *were* to forget how to be a king . . . if you were to command
me to do this outlandishly silly thing, you know perfectly well that I'd refuse.
(240)

Philip is astonished. Ana has so wounded his *amour-propre* that he fails
to hear the wisdom of her words. He is consumed with thoughts

of the love and licence taken here by another man, a commoner; thoughts of
the fool he had made of himself in coming here as to a refuge that was his
own; thoughts of a day . . . when he had sat here in blind man's innocence
between the two, thinking himself almost her lover then, almost her tempter,
giving them reason to laugh at him together afterwards, in their cunningly stolen
delight. (249)

In their climactic conversation, Philip tells Ana that he has intercepted
letters to her from Antonio that prove their liaison. Indignant, Ana denies
his right, even as head of state, to 'steal and read another person's letters'
(251). In this act, more than any other, Philip has brutally disappointed
her. Ana here becomes a very thinly disguised Kate O'Brien. It is the
king's interfering with private correspondence, his intruding on
personal expression, that most offends Ana. As a powerful symbol of
public interference in private matters, the stolen love letters merge with
Kate O'Brien's censored novels. Here, perhaps most dramatically, Kate
O'Brien is at her most subjective; here Ana's rage is Kate O'Brien's most
stirring outburst against the banning of her books. This Ana seems far
removed from sixteenth-century Europe and the motivations of the
emotionally extravagant Princess of Eboli bequeathed by history.

Even after Philip has sentenced her to life imprisonment, the Ana
of *That Lady* continues her crusade for personal and political freedom.
A captive in her own home, she speaks out against despotism. She pleads
simultaneously for Spain and for a Europe free of Fascism and Nazism:

We who had the power, who owned Castile and governed it by the free wisdom
of our people, we sold ourselves to [Philip's] old father — and we have allowed
him to be such a tyrant as Charles never was. I know Philip and I — I have
always loved him, oddly enough. But he is a dangerous tyrant, and we have
been bullied, and here we are, in chaos. The decaying mistress of the world . . .
(316).

Thus, when she is told that her promise never to see Antonio again will secure her freedom, Ana refuses. She explains her position to Cardinal Quiroga, who has been allowed to visit her: 'My soul cannot admit [Philip's] right or anyone's to ask such things of me, let alone put me in prison until I answer them to his liking . . . I cannot countenance blackmail' (322). As before, Kate O'Brien uses the cardinal's response to emphasise the morality of Ana's position:

this stand of yours against blackmail is one of Spain's few good deeds at present — and I for one am glad to witness it . . . [You] are fighting quite simply for your idea of human conduct. If you've done wrong in the past — and you have — your are now doing something that is hard and right and cold and even disinterested. Moreover, you are acting in character. (322-3).

The cardinal's words are the highest praise. Ana has fulfilled her own goal — and Kate O'Brien's goal as a novelist — to create 'life in action'.

Cardinal Quiroga, whom she portrays as unusually humane and enlightened for his time, also emphasises Kate O'Brien's interpretation of Philip's possessive love. As Kate O'Brien depicts him, Philip's feelings for Ana are stronger even than his concern for affairs of state. Jealousy alone, she claims, not the treasonable acts that some historians have suggested,[16] force Philip to imprison Ana and Antonio. While Philip's jealousy is very much in keeping with one dimension of his personal legend, it reflects Kate O'Brien's long-standing concern with love that is narcissistic and egocentric, with the malignant possessiveness that confuses itself with love.

As Ana navigates the course that makes her most herself, Philip's wish to control her intensifies. The cardinal explains Philip to Ana and the reader. Philip has, he says,

no claim on the private life of either of you — but as your king, on his own terms, he has power over you. Since he learnt that you were lovers, he has not been able to be quite quit of the thought of either or both of you. And he has got his miserable personal emotion entangled with the Escovedo problem — because somehow hidden in that may be, if he can find it, the destruction of your lover. And it isn't that he's in love with you. It's that he has long been in love with the idea of your being in love with him. (321)

Kate O'Brien suggests that Ana's years of suffering lie in Philip's insane jealousy, in his psychopathology. As Philip's possession, Ana is his narcissistic extension. His love is not love, 'even at love's crudest. It's self-love, insanely indulged by a lonely and unbalanced man' (322). Ana matters so much to him only because she is all that is 'left of the days of pride of [Philip's] life' (108).

Philip's stigmatised love is balanced by the adoration between Ana and her youngest child Anichu, the only comfort that Philip allows Ana in her incarcreration. The Princess of Eboli in fact was accompanied in her confinement by her *eldest* daughter, also named Ana, whose life following her mother's death parallels Anichu's.[17] By making this devoted child the *youngest* of Ana's children, Kate O'Brien, the youngest daughter in her family, marks Ana's story once again as unmistakably her own. It is not surprising, considering what we know of Kate O'Brien, that after all Ana has suffered, she should return to that relationship which, even more than her love for Antonio, has given her the deepest satisfaction. Children shine radiantly through most of Kate O'Brien's works, and parent-child affection is frequently the one she renders most movingly. But Anichu basks in special sunlight. Ana's maternal joy is a brilliant contrast to the curse of Philip's love. For Ana, now confined to her home, being 'with the child . . . to love her and enjoy her love, was indeed a poignant consolation and almost a stronger attachment to life than any other she had ever felt' (360-61). She worries, though, that the longer they live together now, 'the wider and more wounding would be [Anichu's] grief when Ana died, and the harder her return to normal life . . . to the ways and friends of her own generation' (361). Ana knows that she has been Anichu's 'one great love' (361). Has the child not said, 'I won't marry. I prefer to stay with you . . . What I love is being with you' (341)? Ana contrasts markedly not only with Philip but with Anthony Considine and Hannah Kernahan. In her generosity of spirit, she most resembles Mère Marie-Hélène and her devotion to Anna Murphy.

Philip, in his vengeance, has stripped Ana of everything except her child, but Ana and Anichu have both chosen their lots. Here are selfless love and selfhood, choice and conviction, imprisoned by absolute, arbitrary power. The darkness that envelops Ana as she awaits death is Kate O'Brien's bleakest symbol yet for what befalls the woman who demands independence, but Ana conquers the night, the love between her and her child illuminating her sacrifice. When Ana dies, she is buried in Pastrana. Her search for her self has led her home and to her child, for Anichu returns to the convent there as a Franciscan postulant. She never leaves her mother.

Kate O'Brien ends the novel by reasserting the historical consequence of Philip's destructive love. Now old and sick, he is surrounded by images of his failure to his faith, to his nation, and to himself. As he reflects on lost opportunities, his thoughts alight on Ana, 'his most private' (375) discomfort, and he remembers how much he had loved and admired her, how much she had hurt and humiliated him. Now, after so many years of imprisonment and five months after her death,

Ana still hurts him 'more . . . than he could bear'. Ana's cause wounded her, but it has wounded Philip more. He will never 'master the leaden, deadly pain in his breast' (378) that is her legacy. Ana's struggle to control her private life and her unwillingness to yield it to Philip's demands have affected him more than all the battles of faith and empire he has waged. In the end, Ana has won. For Philip, the loss of the Armada was an easier defeat.

Nine

The Flower of May

That Lady is so mature, so sure and sound that it might well have been Kate O'Brien's last fiction. But after returning to Ireland in 1949 to settle in Roundstone, Co. Galway, Kate O'Brien wrote two more novels. Far less successful than *That Lady,* these works similarly address the large issue of social defiance embodied in Ana de Mendoza. They also sound a theme muted but tenacious throughout her collective work. Homosexual love — implied in *The Flower of May,*[1] overt in *As Music and Splendour*[2] — becomes Kate O'Brien's most dramatic symbol for the outcast, the unconventional individual.

In her final novels, Kate O'Brien describes more fully the love that she could only intimate in her earlier works. The bonds between Denis Considine and Tony Lanigan, and between Denis and Flasher Devoy in *Without My Cloak,* the infatuation of Agatha Conlon with Mary Lavelle, Professor Archer's affair with Etienne in *The Land of Spices,* and Anna Murphy's prophetic, transforming vision of Pilar in that same novel, all prefigure the relationships of Fanny Morrow and Lucille de Mellin in *The Flower of May* and of Clare Halvey and Luisa Carriaga in *As Music and Splendour.*

Published in 1953 and 1958 respectively, Kate O'Brien's last novels recapitulate the evolution of feminine erotic love as it appeared in women's literature of the past two centuries, from the unselfconsciously passionate, if not necessarily physical, attachments of nineteenth-century women to the explicitly sexual relationships of twentieth-century lesbians. Even within the context of the development of fiction about lesbianism in the twentieth century, a context in which Kate O'Brien is sill unrecognised, *The Flower of May* and *As Music and Splendour* are remarkable, one for its atavistic portrayal of sexual innocence, the other for its avant-garde engagement with sexual difference. As fiction, these novels are flawed, perhaps because Kate O'Brien knows too much: the innocence she describes in *The Flower of May* has long since passed, and the acceptance for which she pleads in *As Music and Splendour* is yet to come. As a record of lesbianism in literature, however, these take the reader from the first veiled stirrings of female homosexuality to the unabashed expression of love between women.

In *The Flower of May,* Kate O'Brien moves back in space to Ireland and in time to 1907 — her tenth year. As she did in the roughly contemporaneous *The Land of Spices,* she portrays the origins of the creative sensibility through an intelligent ingenue. But the heroine of *The Flower of May* emphasises a personal dimension that Kate O'Brien only lightly sketched in the story of Anna Murphy. Anna is supported in her choice of education and in her development as an artist by the loving Reverend Mother at *La Couvent de la Sainte Famille.* Eighteen-year-old Fanny Morrow, however, enjoys a passionate friendship with Lucille de Mellin, an older student at the Belgian mother-house of *La Couvent.* Together, they pursue the same goals Anna had established. Fanny, however, has yet to realise the significance of her preference for Lucille's companionship over either of Lucille's eligible brothers — and over anyone else. The meaning of Fanny's desire remains as much a mystery to her, though certainly not to the reader, as the secret Lucille promises to tell but never does. Lucille's manner suggests that the secret is that she knows she is a lesbian. But Fanny, despite the understanding and maturity that she acquires as she watches her beloved mother die and as she intervenes in her newly-wed sister's infidelity, remains surprisingly naive about herself. She never acknowledges that her love for Lucille may be sexual or erotic.

With 'very extraordinary tact and sensitivity',[3] Kate O'Brien indicates that Fanny and Lucille's relationship far exceeds the adolescent *Schwärm* she whimsically illustrated in *The Land of Spices.* No school-girl crush, no passing fancy, it is a serious commitment to a shared life. Fanny and Lucille are remarkably similar to romantic friends of the eighteenth and nineteenth centuries, women who lived within 'erotic love relationship[s] without genital sex'.[4] In England, as well as in America, in a world yet to be analysed by Richard von Krafft-Ebbing, Havelock Ellis, and Sigmund Freud,

close, caring, sensual, and passionate attachments between women were commonplace and accepted . . . Society encouraged the development of these bonds without specifically naming them; thus a woman who loved other women did not have to make her attraction to such intimacies central to her self-definition. Since the ideology of passionlessness . . . constructed women as nonsexual beings, they could participate in tender, even sensual bonds without viewing their love as sexual.[5]

In *Surpassing the Love of Men,* Lillian Faderman summarises the explanations of feminist scholars for the phenomenon in which Fanny Morrow and Lucille de Mellin participate:

Because throughout much of the nineteenth century in Britain and America, sex was considered an activity in which virtuous women were not interested and did not indulge unless to gratify their husbands and to procreate, it was generally inconceivable to society that an otherwise respectable woman could choose to participate in a sexual activity that had as its goal neither procreation nor pleasing a husband. Because there was seemingly no possibility that women would want to make love together, they were permitted a latitude of affectionate expression and demonstration that became more and more narrow with the growth of general sophistication and pseudosophistication regarding sexual possibilities between women. (152)

In addition to its apparent sexual innocence, the bond between Fanny and Lucille demonstrates other characteristics typical of documented romantic friendships in the eighteenth and nineteenth centuries. At that time such female friends sought 'blissful [lives]together',[6] in which each would control her destiny; each would relate to the other as an adult in a way precluded by 'a heterosexual relationship with a virtual stranger (often . . . a much older man), arranged by a parent for considerations totally divorced from affection'.[7] To escape what seemed a pre-ordained imprisonment, such couples established homes together and made sacrifices to secure them.[8] Similarly, Fanny and Lucille, separated socially and economically from their families, achieve what feminist historians have defined as the personal goals of the first generation of 'New Women' who emerged during the second half of the nineteenth century. They avoid traditional female roles, reject their mothers' domesticity, and elude the subjugation of personal fulfilment to bourgeois properties'.[9]

Occupied throughout her career with the social positions of women, Kate O'Brien frequently embraced the *Bildungsroman,* of which *The Land of Spices, Mary Lavelle* and *As Music and Splendour* are examples. But, though Fanny and Lucille embark on an unconventional course, liberating themselves from the communal expectations that would constrain them, *The Flower of May* eludes the designation. It neither explores nor exploits the awakening to self-knowledge that estranges the individual from society. Fanny's search for values other than those 'defined by love and marriage'[10] yields no greater understanding of herself or of the power of the society that limits her. As the book ends, Fanny is still unaware that her feelings for Lucille are sexual. Describing the typical femal novel of development, Susan J. Rosowski underscores the uncharacteristic innocence of *The Flower of May:*

The direction of awakening follows what is becoming a pattern in literature by and about women: movement is inward, toward greater self-knowledge that leads in turn to a revelation of the disparity between self-knowledge and the nature of the world. The protagonist's growth results typically not with 'an art of living', as for her male counterpart, but instead with a realisation that for a woman such an art of living is difficult or impossible: it is an awakening to limitations.[11]

Fanny's persistent naïveté and blindness to the truth about herself imparts to *The Flower of May* the quality of a romantic fairy tale. The novel is Kate O'Brien's dream of perpetual innocence — the innocence of an earlier era that still considered love between women natural, that knew it only as devoted friendship. In *The Flower of May,* the 'ideology of passionlessness',[12] of women as non-sexual beings, still prevails; thus, the female characters express same-sex love without thinking themselves abnormal. Kate O'Brien presents a pre-lapsarian romantic friendship almost nostalgically as her characters create 'their own nurturing world of "love and ritual" in a sexually polarized society'.[13] The only evil is misguided heterosexuality; the heroines of this novel believe that, by turning their backs on the convention of marriage, they can escape the disappointments that beset their conformist sisters.

Kate O'Brien indulges in the hope that Fanny and Lucille, and women like them, can be free from the anguish that was inherent in the liaisons of her heterosexual characters. Consequently, the novel becomes a prelude to *As Music and Splendour,* in which the author will paint the homosexual dimension of her characters with greater realism and indicate that love between women is no more perverse and no less painful than heterosexual love. In *The Flower of May* Kate O'Brien mutedly eroticises female bonding as it occurs between friends, between family members, and between teachers and pupils, and its consequences are always benign. In *As Music and Splendour,* Clare Halvey will suffer as much for her love as Mary Lavelle suffered for hers.

Kate O'Brien's first tacit exploration of lesbian life recasts the story of Anna Murphy's artistic evolution. But *The Flower of May* speculates on the fate of a young heroine who has the emotional and financial means as well as a companion with whom to escape family, country, and convention. Must this young woman confront the blows that stung so many of Kate O'Brien's previous characters? The author seems here to think not. With an inheritance from her aunt to sustain her and with Lucille de Mellin at her side, Fanny Morrow foresees a productive future with which Kate O'Brien's narrative seems to concur. Unlike Stephen Dedalus, Fanny need not abandon her Cranly. With Lucille, she leaves Ireland and her youth, experiencing little of Anna's (or, for that matter, of Stephen's) anxiety. *The Flower of May* is Kate O'Brien's dream vision, a feminist idyll of artistic beginnings.

In reconsidering the female artist's adolescence, Kate O'Brien calls up, in addition to Anna Murphy, characters who grow immediately from her other novels. Familiar situations and themes also reappear. The power of the family is still crucial, and again, Kate O'Brien treats it ambiguously. The loving ties that bind Fanny's mother and aunt, Julia Morrow and Eleanor Delahunt, for example, are profound. Yet, in their mutual devotion, each woman tenderly, unwittingly, robs the other of a fulfilling maturity. Julia's marriage to Joseph Morrow and their move to Dublin precluded Eleanor's entrance into the order of *Sainte Famille*. She had to remain in Clare to care for her father and to farm Glasalla, the sisters' childhood home. Still, Eleanor's love so insulates Julia and binds her to Glasalla that despite the span of years and miles, she can never emotionally leave it. At Glasalla, time stands still, and childhood is eternal. Julia perpetually refers to Glasalla as 'home' and moves through her life in Dublin as if in a dream. She sees to her daily routines and obligations and is cherished by all who know her, and yet, as the family's old friend Canon Whelan puts it, Julia's 'never been all here. Anyhow, never all in Dublin' (15). Leaving Glasalla, Kate O'Brien suggests, represents more than growing up and leaving home. The exodus from childhood is tantamount to exile; both lead to the painful rootlessness that so many of Kate O'Brien's characters, as well as the author herself, have endured.

But, for all its resemblances to her earlier novels, *The Flower of May* is most akin to *The Land of Spices*. Both come closest to being her *Künstlerroman,* a version of the narrative of Kate O'Brien's own development as novelist and woman. In each, a young woman asserts her right to, and moves towards, the intellectual, artistic life. We first meet Fanny just after she has left *La Compagnie de Sainte Famille,* ready to continue her education at a university. Her grasping for independence and self-determination evokes and continues the younger Anna Murphy's journey. Although Fanny's familial and social milieux are happier and more comfortable than Anna's, the limitations and demands are similar. Each encounters the formidable claims of family that have been reinforced by social convention. Perhaps not consciously, each also wishes to become a writer, and Kate O'Brien suggests that Fanny's childhood memories will, like Anna's and her own, provide the basis for forthcoming fiction. 'So fixed was childhood . . . so present always the past. Fanny knew the idiom and had nothing against it. Yet she watched it, as she grew up, from outside. She watched it lovingly — yet as a novelist might' (38). Once again, Kate O'Brien's ambivalence surfaces as she contrasts the insider's loving perception with the outsider's critical view.

While she has tempered the social satire in *The Flower of May*, the author continues both to trivialise the Irish Catholic bourgeoisie and to revile its latent destructiveness. Though the Morrows are comfortably ensconced in the Irish middle class, the family's fortunes are in decline, not nearly to the extent of Anna Murphy's, but sufficiently so that Joseph Morrow can pay only for Fanny's sister Lilian's wedding and not for her own schooling. Still, the mores that dominate her life are more invidious to Fanny's future than are her finances; not only are weddings and trousseaux of greater value to a woman than education, but, also, a sentimental father can insist that his favourite daughter, his 'flower of May', sacrifice the schooling she craves and live at home:

angry, resentful though she might be, training would and did prevail — and if she lived in her father's house and ate his bread, and loved him and her mother, she would naturally behave as a daughter and as a disciplined person, who has learnt, and who understands, that her transitory desires are not paramount. (29)

Fanny's conventional father and other-worldly mother are blind to her emotional and intellectual needs. They envision a life for her similar to her sister's: an appropriate marriage and a home near them in Dublin. The toast at her wedding would be like the 'unfortunate enunciation' offered at Lilian's: 'I wish you health, I wish you joy, and every year a bouncing boy' (3). Fanny accedes momentarily, but she knows that the arrangement will be untenable: 'In a sentence Fanny had been instructed to understand that home was enough; and she had instantly apprehended, even as her father spoke . . . that it was not' (34). Feeling trapped, Fanny can only wait.

To rescue Fanny from such confinement, however, Eleanor Delahunt gives her the deeds to Glasalla. Explaining her gift, Aunt Eleanor sounds remarkably like Mère Marie-Hélène arguing in *The Land of Spices* with Anna Murphy's grandmother about the girl's future:

I believe my niece to have some powers, some intellectual talents, which will have to be educated. The father has neither the means nor the desire to give her such freedom of education. He has sons, he is not rich, and he is selfish and sentimental about this daughter.
    . . . I desire my niece to have in her hand as from today a weapon of independence which she will use or not, as she may choose, in the immediate years, not to say months.
    . . . [Glasalla] is unencumbered . . . she can encumber it, surely, if she likes . . . to educate herself? (153-4)

In both novels, older women come to the aid of younger protégées. Kate O'Brien suggests a feminine, not masculine, line of strength and continuity. The aunt, who herself had been forced into a life of self-denial and sacrifice, identifies with the niece. As Mère Marie-Hélène interceded to liberate Anna Murphy, so Eleanor intercedes to liberate Fanny.

But even before Glasalla is transferred, Kate O'Brien indicates that Fanny will deviate from family expectations; Fanny, we are told, has 'no intention of going Lilian's way, and her mind would not long be contained between the two bridges that span the canal at either end of Mespil Road' (30). Persistently, the author suggests the pending familial struggle. While journeying though Northern Italy with Lucille and the de Mellin brothers, her first taste of freedom, Fanny speaks portentously of her wish 'to have no relations whom one loves and to whom one owes the normal considerations of love, and to have instead of them a little secret nest egg — just enough to go off quietly and get some decent education and sort things out' (157-8). Furthermore, her need to be different draws Fanny towards individuals whose defiance of convention has ostracised them from the Catholic bourgeoisie — her mother's cousin Lady Rawlinson, for example, who is judged a 'pervert' because she married a Protestant. Fanny's curiosity about Lady Rawlinson is aroused as she wonders 'wherein lay the rights and wrongs of that long-ago decision . . . which was indeed a defiance of fixed doctrine, and which still, after thirty years, disturbed social relations? What was the general reference from the private action?' (23). As a woman, Fanny will choose a non-traditional life with Lucille; as a writer, she will continue, as her creator did, to seek the 'general reference in the private action'.

Others, though certainly not her parents, recognise Fanny's distinctiveness. Cousin Bill, who remains remarkably perceptive despite his drinking, sees this difference and envisions her 'future in bourgeois society somewhat uneasily' (47). At Lilian's wedding, with which Kate O'Brien opens the novel, Fanny seems to him 'out of place' (13), an 'annoyance' (14). Bill senses what will soon be clear: marriage is not at all on Fanny's mind. The reader, too, senses the difference between the sisters when, after a wedding guest refers to 'young Fanny' as 'in the market now', Fanny pointedly slips from 'her father's light hold' (12). As the newly-weds leave for their honeymoon in a Mercedes-Benz, Fanny remarks, 'I'd love to be driving off in that contraption . . . by myself' (5). And we soon learn that paradoxically Fanny has taken a vow to take no vows, neither marital nor religious.

Lucille, too, has resolved to remain single, committed to their shared goals, and foresees the potential for hardship even more clearly than does Fanny. As constrained by her wealth as Fanny is by her lack of it, Lucille eschews her family's aristocratic propensities in favour of her education: 'I will not live my one precious, small life in the way Mother has lived hers. I can't alter the family way of life, or its assumptions

— all I can do is choose a way which will disassociate me from all that, and set me free . . . all [I] know is that [I] desperately require education' (159). She explains her quest to Mère Générale, who has remained utterly devoted to both her star pupils:

by the time I *am* somewhat educated, I'll be a grown-up woman, and Father will have been growing a little used to my foibles, perhaps. I don't know in the least what I shall want to do then — but I'll have started, and I'll have some equipment. I want to go to some foreign university . . .
   I'm determined to live my *own* way . . . It's not important, but it is my intention. (163-4)

Not only are Fanny and Lucille Kate O'Brien's most explicitly feminist characters, they are, thus far, unique. In them we see the connection Kate O'Brien makes between female independence and the rejection of heterosexuality. Implicit in their portrayal as individuals and as passionate friends is the idea that, to be really autonomous, they must both avoid marriage and forge a bond with each other. And although Fanny is briefly drawn to André and Patrice, Lucille's brothers, it is only because they so strongly resemble Lucille. Lucille never wavers in her allegiance to Fanny, and Fanny's distraction is only fleeting. Each knows that, if they are to be independent, they must belong only to each other:

Lucille heard the withheld shake in Fanny's voice. She took the hand that had ruffled her hair, and kissed it lightly.
   'I'm always with you, Fan,' she said.
   Fanny's hand fell away gently. She was almost asleep . . . 'Don't marry anyone, Lucille —'
   'Wasn' it nice, what *Mère Générale* said to us the other day?'
   'You mean: I'll be disappointed if either of you two does the obvious thing?'
   'Yes. I wonder how many of the possible things she would call "obvious"?' (110)

Each vocally disdains the idea of the other's marrying: 'Would you *like* me to marry your brother?' Lucille came and took Fanny's head into her hands. 'No, I'd loathe it' . . . Fanny kissed the lovely, frowning face, smiled into the brilliant, sapphire eyes' (64). Similarly Fanny rejects the idea of Lucille's marrying a German aristocrat:

'You're smiling, Lucille, aren't you?'
   'Yes. How did you know?'
   'I felt it somehow. What are you smiling at?'
   'I think I'm laughing, really. How would I look, Fan, married to Otto van Langenberg?'
   Fanny turned on her pillow and searched Lucille's profile outlined against the gleaming summer midnight.

'You'd look magnificent', she said half amusedly, half in fear. (109)

Fanny and Lucille's behaviour towards each other and their attitudes toward heterosexual relationships are never explicitly identified by Kate O'Brien as lesbian. She does, however, gently blur conventional feminine expectations in her descriptions of the two women. For example, she introduces Lucille in phallic terms; we first see her blond, aryan, standing 'tall and shining' on the 'lordly terrace' (53) of the opulent Villa des Glycines. And when Patrice is about to express his love for Fanny, Kate O'Brien writes, 'Lucille sat on the flat balustrade, and in her gold dress, her long legs crossed, her gold hair catching moonlight, she looked, Fanny thought, like some androgynous myth' (182), hinting that Lucille will assume the role in Fanny's life for which Patrice yearns. Kate O'Brien also describes Fanny's charms ambiguously. Our first view of her is through Cousin Bill's eyes; he sees her beauty as elusive and out of focus, as having a 'mermaid quality . . . She's like what you take in your arms in bed when she isn't there' (4). So saying, Bill has presaged the outcome of Fanny's friendship with Patrice and of her short-lived flirtation with the elder André.

All the relationships between women in *The Flower of May* are stronger and more profound than those between men and women. Heterosexual romantic love, an alluring illusion in Kate O'Brien's previous novels, has become here either sentimental pathos or deceptive evil. In *The Flower of May* none of the masculine characters is the equal of any of the women; not even Patrice de Mellin, a youthful idealist and perhaps Kate O'Brien's most sympathetic male, can rival his sister. Like Richard Froude and Antonio Perez, Patrice embodies Kate O'Brien's disbelief in the power of masculine affection. His expression of love for Fanny comprises some of her least affecting writing:

'Patrice!' Fanny said softly. 'Patrice, why are you crying?' . . .
'Because you are going away, Fanny; because I love you. That is why I weep. My situation is absurd, I know; but I know that neither you nor Lucille will mock at it . . . I am sorry you found me crying, but I am not sorry to have been able to say to you, before Lucille, that I love you. I know you will remember that I said it'. . . .
'Oh dearest boy, dear friend!' she said. (182-3)

Fanny and Patrice, both weeping, know she will never fulfil his love, but neither knows why. His renunication of Fanny permits him to send the two young women off together: 'you and Fanny both go indoors now, please. We'll meet tomorrow for good-by' (183).

With his resemblance to Lucille as his most distinguishing feature, Patrice offers Lucille little competition for Fanny's affection. As Fanny tells Lucille, Patrice is 'good — like you. Not *as* good, perhaps — but good' (308). The elder de Mellin brother, André, however, is not good, as Fanny is slow to recognise. Like Patrice, André looks like Lucille; his eyes are 'exactly' like hers, the *'best* eyes' Fanny had 'seen so far in the world' (308), and she is attracted to the manly André even more than to the boyish Patrice. In indulging her feelings, however, Fanny merely toys with him. She aptly assesses her pleasure in his kiss as the pleasure of her own independence, rather than of his masculinity. Gradually, Fanny sees the vast differences between André and the sister he so strongly resembles. When André seduces Fanny's sister on her honeymoon and almost ruins her marriage, Fanny, empowered by her inheritance, blackmails him for his treachery. She banishes him from Ireland, from her life, and from the book: 'I can expose you, even if I have to do what is called disgrace myself. I'm quite well-off . . . I own Glasalla . . . and I draw an income from it . . . so I can create any sort of scandal I like — and then go off to Italy or Spain or wherever I choose' (335). André's selfishness, vanity, and exploitation enable Fanny to overcome the temptation of heterosexuality, which he represents. Her eventual acknowledgement of André's wickedness — — he is the only wholly despicable figure in Kate O'Brien's canon — clears the way for the life she will lead with Lucille.

Characters in Kate O'Brien's earlier novels who give up heterosexual passion retreat into the family. Fanny, however, overcomes the temptation to loll passively, like her mother, amid the familiar. She dreads such emotional and intellectual confinement, but were it not for her aunt's wisdom and generosity, she would have been consigned to caring for her father after Julia's death. An inept, sentimental man, Joseph Morrow would impede his daughter as her aunt would abet her. Although well-intentioned, he is a bumbler, incapable of managing on his own. Kate O'Brien articulates Fanny's perception of her father's vacuity:

As she watched him . . . boasting a shade too much about his reception at the office — which had obviously restored, but also somewhat pathetically inflated him, she began to feel again the impatience she had customarily felt against him until her mother had died. His bewildered misery then . . . had made her respect him. But, as he crept back to normality . . . to his place as an indispensable businessman and a citizen whose voice and counsel would be missed, Fanny saw all the miserable consolations of empty vanity inflating the poor man again . . . And she saw why Aunt Eleanor, impatient and high bred, had never been able finally to accept Julia's love of Joseph. Eleanor had never understood . . . how Mother could bear his silly little vanities . . . Fanny, thinking bitterly of the day as it had been for her, and as it had been for her mother in her cold coffin in Crahore, had an impulse of unjust anger against her father, and thought with longing of Aunt Eleanor, lonely, grieving in Glasalla. (339-40)

It is not surprising that, in acknowledging her father's weaknesses, Fanny should recall the lonely, dauntless Eleanor, whose self-denial and resolve command the reader's admiration, as well as Fanny's. Eleanor's relationship with Julia is the most durable of this novel. It is a model for the affection between Fanny and Lucille, whose mutual passion is as sisterly as it is romantic. The Delahunt sisters represent, in many respects, that paradigm of love we have seen before in Kate O'Brien's novels. Deeper and more intense than the love between spouses or between heterosexual lovers, the love among family members, about which Kate O'Brien writes the most persuasively, may be the only one in which she truly believes. Nevertheless, the depiction of Eleanor and Julia's love retains her customary awareness of its bitter price. As Eleanor tells Lucille:

The person I have loved most on earth, I think, was my sister Julia. But I did not *admire* her in everything. I loved her — and not merely because she was my only sister and because sisters are assumed to love each other . . . I could easily have hated her for being my sister, had I found her a distasteful person. But I found her lovely, and . . . untarnished by 'the world's slow stain' . . . Nevertheless, I didn't unmitigatedly admire her . . .

I did not understand the life she chose . . . Anyhow my judgment is questionable, because had she chosen either of the two good local suitors she had . . . I could have gone to Place des Ormes . . .

But Julia chose Joseph and Dublin, so I took on Father and Glasalla . . . I always resented that she never once questioned what her choice cost me. Never once, in all our life. (297-8)

Kate O'Brien makes all too certain that the parallels between aunt and niece are explicit. Like Eleanor, Fanny, too, seeks education and independence, but is constrained by her sister's marriage and her parents' wishes. The aunt's generosity will spare the niece a life in which her pleasures are reduced to two cigarettes and a sherry in the privacy of her study each night.

Unlike Julia, Fanny will not be tied to the past. She focuses outward. Nevertheless, Glasalla will become a fixture in her life, and the lighthouse that stands just off the rocks that separate Glasalla from the sea — the 'last glimpse of Erin' they called it — will become as natural to her as it had been to her mother, though in a very different way. Early in the novel, Fanny suggests the depth of communion she will experience with its once repugnant light: 'Why shrink from an ordeal which swung back ruthlessly in every minute from sunset until sunrise?

Almost as foolish to deny the beats of one's own heart' (51). As Julia and Eleanor were bound to and bound by Glasalla and the lighthouse, its light flashing the rhythm of home, so will Fanny respond:

Aunt Eleanor would be in charge [of Glasalla] for many years yet, and by the time she, Fanny, was alone with it, she would have educated herself, made money in some way, and considered how to take charge of Glasalla. However, already as she sat on the wall above the sea and looked from the fierce lighthouse beam back to the dim lights of the house, she understood that henceforward all her studies, hopes and dreams would be anchored to her responsibility for Glasalla. (232)

Fanny will first be free to travel, to watch the world, and to become involved with it as intimately as she pleases. Early in the novel, Lucille had asked 'you wouldn't rule out life outside the family span, would you?' (90). Fanny had responded negatively. Now Fanny knows that choice is a safe one; Glasalla will provide her the freedom she craves and the rootedness she needs.

Fanny's new life will be as different from Anna Murphy's as from Julia's. She sets out, with neither mate nor sibling but with Lucille at her side, for Paris, her *bachot,* and the Sorbonne. With this union, Kate O'Brien can promise her heroine a bright future. Fanny takes 'warmth and help from Lucille's murmuring love, and from some promise of power and growth a part of her answered within Lucille's embrace' (308). Lucille consoles her during her mother's death and funeral:

Therefore, sitting together in the little cell, the two grew gently back to their constant certainty, and Fanny lost the sense of being on the edge of delirium which had possessed her all day.
  'Oh! You're making me feel strong!' she said.
  'You'll need to feel strong, darling', said Lucille. (270)

With the fates of Fanny and Lucille joined, *The Flower of May* ends optimistically; Agatha Conlon, tormented in her hopeless, guilt-ridden love for Mary Lavelle, has no counterpart here.

The reader would like to believe in this promise of evolving female autonomy, but the narrative is not convincing. Kate O'Brien pays an artistic price for even the implicit presentation of forbidden love; artificiality compromises the characters and themes of this novel. The reworking of old elements in a new sexual context is, finally, an unhappy mixture of nostalgia and sentimentality, a melange of too many unrealistic relationships and too few compelling characterisations. In *The Flower of May* secondary figures fall short: although Eleanor Delahunt is one of Kate O'Brien's most masterful creations, the portraits of the dreamy Julia and her sentimental husband languish as mere stereotypes. Lucille's brother André is, like Patrice, disappointing; he appears as a flat, two-dimensional villain in his self-centred exploitation of innocence. Minor characters become caricatures: the German aristocrat Frau von Langenberg and her son and the Irish housekeepers in Dublin and Glasalla, for example. Nor are the family portraits, whether healthy or noxious, as successful as they were in Kate O'Brien's other works. The delight in the accoutrements of good living that had been a part of her earlier novels, Kate O'Brien parodies here to extravagant excess.

The greatest shortcoming is that the supposedly perfect friendship between Fanny and Lucille never really comes to life; it is only etched. Too often sentiment takes the place of feeling. Fanny and Lucille profess their devotion to one another and acknowledge their compatibility, but frequently their dialogue seems little more than fatuous clucking. 'Dearest', 'pet', they call each other. Too much of their emotional life is left hidden, and we never experience the depth of feeling that each alleges for the other. The novel's failure to realise fully its protagonists and their relationship robs it of power and credibility. Its illusory qualities cannot escape the reader's scepticism, and the primary characters, no matter how prettily painted, seem destined for the same disillusionment that befell Kate O'Brien's heterosexual heroines. As *The Flower of May* ends, we still know too little of Fanny and Lucille to accept Kate O'Brien's halcyon vision of their future.

The outcome that Mère Générale predicts for Fanny, though unhappy, may be truer to Kate O'Brien's pattern than the novel's tentative conclusion. As Mère Générale tells Lucille:

Fanny is almost amusingly like her mother — dear, dreaming Julia. And I'd rather she took the simple path of domestic happiness, as Julia surprised us by doing, than weave her secret spirit into some cocoon of pain that no one but she will ever know about. That would not be good, it would be wasteful. (165)

It is this secret 'cocoon of pain' that we associate with Kate O'Brien's mercilessly self-observant heroines and imagine for the author herself. This is the emotional state she draws most frequently and most poignantly. We wish Fanny's friendship with Lucille could preclude that self-protective, self-induced isolation, but Kate O'Brien's intelligence and analysis of human nature is too acute and too shrewd to maintain this utopian vision. As *Music and Splendour* shows us, the pain of companionships such as Fanny and Lucille's is no less hurtful than the struggles Kate O'Brien has already described. *The Flower of May*, in its story and its literary merit, remains merely an unfulfilled promise. It is Kate O'Brien's wishful thinking put to paper.

Ten

As Music and Splendour

Kate O'Brien took the title of her final novel, *As Music and Splendour,* from 'When the Lamp Is Shattered', Shelley's tragic lyric on the death of love. The poem's musical similes illumine her work about two young opera singers and their failed loves. But Kate O'Brien explores the world of Italian opera not only to illustrate once again the futility of love, but also to affirm her oneness with her literary creations. Her portrayal of Rose Lennane and Clare Halvey and their relationships to their art implies that, even though her heroines may be based on Marguerite Burke-Sheridan and Margaret Lydon, respectively, as Lorna Reynolds suggests,[1] they are also projections of the writer herself. The role of the artist as outcast and exile parallels the novelist's presentation of homosexuality, which here casts off its protective shell. Rose and Clare rehearse and replay their lives on stage; their professional parts are cues to their personae. Art and life merge to support the argument that the corpus of Kate O'Brien's work is a depiction of her artistic growth and a narrative of her emotional journey.

In 1887, at sixteen years of age, Clare Halvey and Rose Lennane are thrust on the Continent to pursue operatic careers, first in Paris, then in Rome, and then throughout Italy. In a remarkably short time, they attain artistic success, worldly sophistication, and a depth of self-awareness unusual for their years. As they flourish professionally, however, they recognise that their success, though fleeting, may be their only recompense for the nurturing love of mother and grandmother left behind in Ireland. Independence, seemingly the reward of the artistic life, they learn, is an illusion. Singers have little choice or control over their activities, and both Clare and Rose are soon prisoners to their careers. Clare 'saw that the gates had closed on her. She must accept the decision taken over her head' (94). She

had expected life to be a free and wide advance, in proportion to its lack of importance. Now she began to fear that the only freedoms waiting along her regulated path were the small personal ones, of mood, of sensation, of free and easy love and of habits of self-indulgence. All the meaner freedoms, which in truth only meant a narrowing-back into egotism that was frivolous, a self-bound state, a condition of living which might or might not be sinful in the

Church's sense, but which seemed to her, as she faced it, limiting, sad and a disappointment. (138)

An operatic career becomes as restricting as the mores of Catholic Ireland, especially for Rose and Clare, who, though removed from their families, cannot forget the codes of their childhoods, even as they flout them. Like so many of Kate O'Brien's previous heroines, Rose Lennane and Clare Halvey defy the teachings of their faith and the traditions to which they once conformed, and yet they are never really free of the morality they learned as children. Rose perhaps best explains her — and the author's — defiance: 'No delight that her senses could bring her would ever . . . overcome her certainty of wrong-doing when she made love; but neither would that certainty dissuade her from a necessity she found so sweet, in herself and in her lover' (315). For a final time in her fiction Kate O'Brien not only reiterates the instability of romantic love, but, in a more realistic continuation of *The Flower of May,* explores the consequences and limitations of independence.

If not entirely successful, *As Music and Splendour* is distinctive in its straightforward chronicling of a lesbian relationship. In creating artists whose most successful roles seem invariably to express their private, poignant destinies, Kate O'Brien continues to argue that enduring fulfilment in adult love is impossible. Rose, the Desdemona *assoluta* of La Scala, bruised by her heterosexual love, and Clare, tenuously bound to Luisa Carriaga, refute the promise in *The Flower of May* that Fanny and Lucille will sustain their relationship. All love disappoints — lesbian love, no more and no less than heterosexual love.

Kate O'Brien normalises same-sex love by presenting it with the equal portions of objectivity and sensitivity that infuse her presentation of heterosexual love. In *Mary Lavelle* Agatha Conlon's shame over her unrequited affection for Mary seemed far more evocative than Mary's despair over the loss of her brief passion with Juanito, but Clare's love for the unfaithful Luisa Carriaga is hardly more tormented than Rose's youthful love for the French tenor René Chaloux or her more mature attachment to the aristocratic Italian baritone Antonio de Luca. The several strains of love in *As Music and Splendour* provide equal shares of pleasure and punishment. Clare, more private, perhaps, than Rose, but no more contrite about her relationship with Luisa than is Rose about her *amours,* asks, 'Is to love a mistake . . . It can be awkward. It can be silly. But is it really a mistake — to love another person?' (211). Both Rose and Clare know right from wrong and that, in the eyes of the Church, one's love is as sinful as the other's. Kate O'Brien balances her descriptions of the women's self-awareness. Rose, 'like every well-taught Irish child . . . knew her catechism; so she knew where she stood, she knew that she alone was responsible for her sins, and that she had no legitimate consultant outside the confessional box' (313). Clare predicts, 'I don't think I'll ever be the slave of the Penny Catechism, but at the same time I'd find it hard — if I ran into serious moral conflict — I'd find it hard to decide that I was right and the Eternal Church wrong!' (144). She speaks for both of them — and surely for the author — when she tells her fellow student Thomas Evans, who is in love with her:

I am a sinner in the argument of my Church. But so would I be if I were your lover. So is Rose a sinner — and she knows it — in reference to our education and faith. You, who come out of Baptist chapels, don't know how clear our instruction is. Rose and I know perfectly well what we're doing. We are so well instructed that we can decide for ourselves. There's no vagueness in Catholic instruction. (207)

It is ironic that by invoking Church doctrine to reinforce her assertion that heterosexual and homosexual loves follow the same patterns of pleasure and pain, Kate O'Brien normalises Clare's lesbianism for the reader. She insists that we view Clare, the non-conformist, as neither in greater violation of society's decrees, nor as more aggrieved than her other characters. The maid Assunta, for example, is chained in servitude because of a youthful indiscretion with a young man. She is Kate O'Brien's most devastating symbol of the consequence of sexual misconduct, but no more miserable than her drunken mistress, Signora Vittoria. The once-brilliant *diva* is trapped by her narcissism in an unsatisfying marriage with Signor Giacomo, a renowned opera teacher with little left of his self-respect. Their marriage has thwarted creativity and artistic achievement; as the only one we see in the novel, it may represent the institution as a whole, which Kate O'Brien calls one of the 'repetitious monotonies of mature life' (81). In its predictability, marriage appears as troubling as the 'immoral' independence of the unmarried characters.

Kate O'Brien provides us with a range of love in this novel that parallels the range of religious belief in *The Ante-Room*. Except for Signora Vittoria and Signor Giacomo's, all the loves in *As Music and Splendour* are forbidden by Catholic doctrine, and the author presents them all equally without moral condemnation. Luisa Carriaga expresses her affection for her teacher and fellow Spaniard Iago Duarte in an affair that is unimpeded by each of their passions for Clare. Thomas wishes to make love to Clare even though he recognises her feelings for Luisa and has other affairs himself. While still a young priest, Duarte had an affair with the young singer Marie Brunel; his impiety drove her to enter the *Couvent des Pieuses Filles de Sainte Hélène* where she was to become the respected teacher of Europe's greatest singers, including Clare and Rose. Antonio, in love with Rose, has an affair with another student. Amid such promiscuity, Clare feels no more contemptible than those other supposed-sinners. As she explains to Thomas,

> You can argue as you like against my loving Luisa. But I can argue back all your unbridled sins. We all know the Christian rule — and every indulgence of the flesh which does not conform to it is wrong. All right. We are all sinners. You and I and Rose and Tonio and René and Mariana — and all our friends. (208)

If we compare Kate O'Brien's treatment of this lesbian theme with the tradition of novels in the genre, we see more clearly her aesthetic and psychological insight, her ability to see beyond the constrictions of her time and culture. In form, *As Music and Splendour* resembles other novels that explore the development of the lesbian personality: 'formally staid, [evincing] a conventionality that has served both a homosexual and heterosexual audience'.[2] A *Bildungsroman,* the category so 'popular' among novelists who write about 'the extreme outsider among outsiders',[3] it dramatises a young heroine's growth from innocence to experience, her recognition and acceptance of her lesbian feelings, and her realisation that they are taboo. It shares with other novels of this type the view that the heroine's first love is almost invariably 'inadequate or inhibiting', one lover betrays the other either by 'leaving her for a man' or by failing 'to protect her from the vindictive outside world'.[4] Clare's first inkling of her love for Luisa, which has flourished since their days at *Rue des Lauriers,*[5] her Catholic sense of guilt, her knowledge of Luisa's affairs with both Duarte and Julie Constant, and Thomas's attacking her as a 'stinking lily' (209) conform to the formula of the typical lesbian *Bildungsroman.* But, in its hopeful ending, *As Music and Splendour* is remarkably forward-looking. It resembles the novels, written after the women's movement of the 1970s, that promise freedom and/or community to social outcasts.[6] Kate O'Brien rescues her outcasts from their isolation by creating a colony of artists which, though not the 'lesbian culture' that Bonnie Zimmerman envisions (255), and at odds with customary morality, replaces their forsaken homes and families.

According to Catharine Stimpson, Radclyffe Hall's *The Well of Loneliness,* which 'tends to ignore the more benign possibilities of lesbianism' (248), is the prototypical lesbian novel:

> As if making an implicit, perhaps unconscious pact with her culture, the lesbian writer who rejects both silence and excessive coding can claim the right to write for the public in exchange for adopting ... the dying fall, a narrative of

damnation, of the lesbian's suffering as a lonely outcast attracted to a psychological lower caste . . . (247, 244)

This negativism evolved from the aversion to female homosexuality in the twentieth century. Despite a growing tolerance towards voluntary 'non-procreative heterosexuality', there was a keen intolerance of a 'necessarily non-procreative homosexuality, especially if practicing it threatened to mean social as well as sexual self-sufficiency' (245). Both female and male homosexual writers endured such censorship internally as well as externally. Although 'guilt and anxiety rarely appear in homosexual literature until the late nineteenth century . . . [they] become the major theme of *Angst* . . . after 1914' (245).

The further belief that the lesbian is physically sick and deformed, a freak, a member of a third sex, a mannish woman who has no place in the normal biological or social order contributed to this ostracism. In novels that preceded the feminist movement, the lesbian heroine freed herself, as part of her awakening, from prescribed feminine roles by identifying her true self with inherently masculine traits. Stephen Gordon, created by Radclyffe Hall in 1928, became the literary representative of the lesbian writer, just as she became the clinical representative for sexologists, such as Krafft-Ebbing, who fused masculine traits and lesbianism. The mannish lesbian proved so potent an image in the first half of the century that the lesbian 'who did not feel somehow male' was considered an impossibility. The 'womanly lesbian contradicted the convictions that sexual desire must be male and that a feminine woman's object of desire must be a man'.

Written a dozen years before the changes wrought by the feminist movement would be recorded in lesbian literature, *As Music and Splendour* had already moved beyond *The Well of Loneliness*. Although haunted by the spectre of sin, Kate O'Brien's novel is not a parable of the lesbian's damnation. Although Clare suffers for her sexual preference, she is no more unhappy or isolated than the heterosexual Rose, no more plagued by shame, guilt, and self-hatred. Clare accepts herself as a sinner and a lesbian with a quiet peace. By preserving the femininity of both women, Kate O'Brien returns the lesbian to her own sex. Luisa may play Orpheo on stage, but in a further departure from the Stephen Gordon image, she, like Clare, is beautiful, and feminine. In *As Music and Splendour* Kate O'Brien has transcended the suggestion of androgyny in her characterisation of Lucille de Mellin.

Although unique in its prescient balance and objectivity, *As Music and Splendour* is missing from every major history or critical work on literature concerned with lesbianism. Historiographers of the genre seem ignorant even of Kate O'Brien's existence. Lillian Faderman, author of the most comprehensive study of lesbianism in literature, has supported the idea that Radclyffe Hall's Stephen Gordon was the norm and overlooks entirely a work that, in so many ways, is an important alternative to the doctrine of *The Well of Loneliness*. The lesbian image that Clare and Luisa convey is one neither of permanent happiness nor of 'hell or martyrdom', as Lillian Faderman has described Stephen's fate (357). Clare's anguish over her parting from Luisa is no greater than that of the heterosexual Rose, who must also give up her 'immoral' love.

Kate O'Brien's attempt to render homosexuality unexceptional is also apparent in Clare and Luisa's attraction to men. Kate O'Brien's lesbians are not the doomed biological 'invert' of *The Well of Loneliness*, who has no choice in her loves. Clare has satisfying male friendships, and, like Fanny Morrow, finds men physically appealing. Clare very much enjoys Paddy Flynn's company until he becomes fanatically judgmental of her life and her friends. The failed seminarian, who is in love with her, is too harsh a representation of the Irish morality she seeks to escape. While *The Flower of May* offered no positive models of the heterosexual male, Kate O'Brien creates, in this more explicitly lesbian novel, a worthy alternative to same-sex love in Thomas Evans, whose love Clare cherishes but cannot requite. Were it not for Luisa, Clare tells Thomas, 'Easily I might have loved you . . . But — *she* caught my heart before I knew what was happening' (211). Clare wears his bracelet with 'stones like tears' (252) around her wrist while she wears Luisa's chain around her neck. Although she thinks of Thomas as a brother, she is aware that his is a 'kind of brotherliness not in the common competence of brothers' (278) and takes pleasure in her attraction to him. When he once 'took her in his arms and kissed her', Clare 'stayed in the embrace a minute and even he thought that half-wearily she desired to give it back' (179). Clare's attraction to Thomas is not the capitulation to societal demands with which some lesbian novels end; rather, it is Kate O'Brien's insistence that lesbians are open and responsive to other forms of love.

Kate O'Brien suggests that the heroines of *As Music and Splendour* diverge morally and professionally from even their own expectations because their move from Ireland insists on change. Clare muses, 'It often makes me wonder — when you think of how uniform and rule-of-thumb everyone is expected to be at home — I mean, why did they pick you and me to be sent off into the unknown and be re-made, re-fashioned altogether — and at their expense?' (189). As Kate O'Brien's earlier fiction explored the limits and comforts of all the options open to her female characters — marriage, the religious life, exile — in *As Music and Splendour,* the characters themselves imagine the various lives they might have lived. Rose and Clare, both of whom retain loving feelings for home, describe for each other how they would have fared in Ireland. Clare begins:

'But seriously — supposing we'd both been left where we were, I'd have left school in Drumcondra and gone to work, in a shop I suppose, or perhaps dressmaking with Aunt Josie — and you, what would you be doing in Lackanashee?'
'Oh, I'd have gone out earning — in Mellick, I suppose. Maybe in a shop, like you!'
'You might have got married very quickly, of course.'
'So might you.'
'Married, me? Oh no. I *might* have gone to be a nun. But anyway, whatever we did, you'd still be Rose Lennane, your exact, born self, the very girl who was sent to France — only you weren't sent. And I'd be Clare Halvey, as sure as I *am* Clare Halvey. But that Rose Lennane and Clare Halvey there at home, our identical twins, wouldn't be recognisable to us now; to us, I mean, who are trying to imagine them, here in Rome at this minute —'
'But that's true about anyone who, well, who was once definitely parted from herself, her obvious self, at any kind of crossroads. Isn't it?'
'I suppose so. Only it's queer to realise that if I'd stayed at home I'd have — well, played, if you like — one specific character called Clare Halvey all my life — and now, because I came to Italy and learnt to sing, I'll play another one — a creature known on programmes as Chiara Alve, but who simply is Clare Halvey.' (189-90)

In Ireland, Clare would have been saved from unseemliness in the life of a nun where the flesh and spirit, always at war, can be quelled. Like Helen Archer, she sees the religious life in Ireland not entirely as a spiritual calling but as a means of suppressing passion (a phenomenon Kate O'Brien recognised in her Aunt Fan and described in *Presentation Parlour*). As Clare tells Thomas,

I see now some explanation of the tendency of my race — the Irish . . . to become nuns and priests.
. . . [m]any imaginations are too extended to passion. The Irish imagination is a bit lopsided, maybe, [sic] Anyway it isn't at all like the Latin — we are *alarmed* by the power and stretch of feeling . . . We don't find it at all amusing to be in love — that's why we are so awkward. We are not Mediterranean. (209-10)

At home, Rose would have settled down, not as a nun but as a traditional Irish wife; in Italy, however, she accepts the necessity of that 'power and stretch of feeling' that leaves her countrymen 'alarmed'.

She was distant now, in spirit as in space, from those loves on which she had been nourished at home. But Italy and music had educated her temperament as well as her talent. And she knew now, had known for a long time, in silent anxiety, that she must live with love. (134)

As much as their geographies, however, their music informs their lives. Kate O'Brien's transposing of her own personality into the 'disguise of myth' (113) of her fictional narratives is dramatised in the artistic self-expression of the two singers. Violetta, Gilda, Desdemona, Rose's great roles, are all women who sacrifice themselves for love. Each heroine portends the sacrifice that Rose will make for Antonio when she forgoes her life with him once he is engaged to be married. As Norma, Clare is subjected to Pollione's unfaithfulness just as she is to Luisa's; the pair's tragic sacrifice on the opera's funeral pyre represents one fate of Clare's unconventional love. In Gluck's opera, Orfeo is traditionally a travesty role for a mezzo soprano (here, it is Luisa's role); thus, the singing parts suggest the lovers' relationship. Kate O'Brien implies that each woman's destiny is in her art, that their roles reveal their true selves. Of Rose she writes that 'she is *given* to Italian opera . . . she is it, and it is she. She flows in it, and it flows through her' (89). And of Clare and Luisa, playing Eurydice and Orfeo, she writes with similar suggestiveness, 'Still Orpheus and Eurydice, their brilliantly made-up eyes swept for each the other's face, as if to insist that this disguise of myth in which they stood, was their mutual reality, their one true dress wherein they recognised each other' (113).

But Clare is perhaps most fully revealed not in her operatic roles, but in her talent for religious music. Her performance in Pergolesi's *Stabat Mater* is as important to her personally as is *Orfeo,* and, professionally, as is Rose's singing of Desdemona at La Scala. Pergolesi's celebrated hymn that recites the Seven Sorrows of the Virgin at the Cross implies not only her scrupulous, if unconventional, morality but her sacrifice for and distress over her love. Most important, it hearkens to her yearning for her grandmother — a yearning that haunts *As Music and Splendour.* Here, again, Kate O'Brien returns to her melancholy theme that the most enduring love is the love within the family. Even when Kate O'Brien represents characters with fully realised artistic careers and mature, if problematic, sexuality, she insists that their loves from the past are the strongest and most persistent.

Early in the novel, Kate O'Brien offers a personal meditation that reveals her intimate understanding of Clare's loss and attachments:

What she did not know, sixteen years old and looking out in wretched alienation at the rain as it fell on a dull street of Paris — what she did not know then, or ever, that her desire to be back under a rain she knew, among stones and empty lanes, and looking at grey sea and a wet pier, and hearing her grandmother's sweet, good voice calling her in out of the wet to her tea —

she did not know then that in such agony she was meeting one of mankind's least manageable pains. (13)

Throughout the book the motherless Clare hears that call to home unremittingly, and always the promise of her grandmother's comfort calls most strongly. She hears again and again, 'Come in, child . . . Come in out of the wind, my love' (14). Always Clare carries

childhood with her . . . She was well used by now to remembering Grandmother, and the rainy street of Ballykerin and the flapping, clear sea against the wall and the screaming birds and her little curly-headed sisters, fighting and barefoot and always damp and hungry. She carried it all with a cautious quiet now, and sometimes allowed herself to wonder what in fact it held in its sad simplicity, that made it into a precious, secret reliquary, a treasure which she had to conceal and assess only in the dark privacy of waking and going to sleep. What made it gleam so constantly . . . She did not know. But she had learnt to live with its reality. (93-4)

The desire for love governs Clare's behaviour. She yearns for Luisa, away on tour, as she yearns for her grandmother. Clare writes to Luisa that she no longer cries for her 'at awkward moments' but only 'in bed' (196) and explains that her grandmother wrote

that she did not hope to see me again, but that she would be glad if she did, and that often when she was asleep she thought she heard me singing 'My Redeemer liveth' . . . Ah, but Grandmother is wrong! I'll see her again. Please God! . . . I am going to slave between now and next June . . . I'm going home to Ballykerin in June, I'm going to Grandmother. I'm going to sing whatever she wants to hear. And you'll come with me? Will you?' (197)

Though uncertain about the precise significance of the desire for lost maternal love, some feminist theorists see it as a component of same-sex attraction: 'lesbian relationships do tend to recreate mother-daughter emotions and connections'.[7] Supposedly, the lesbian woman wishes to find again, and fuse with, that primary object of her affection. Catharine Stimpson asserts, 'A mother waits at the heart of the labyrinth of some lesbian texts. There she unites past, present, and future. Finding her, in herself, and through a surrogate, the lesbian re-enacts a daughter's desire for the woman to whom she was once so linked, from whom she was then so severed' (256). Adrienne Rich goes further, saying, 'The woman who has felt "unmothered" may seek mothers all her life — may even seek them in men'.[8] The comments pertain to *As Music and Splendour* and, perhaps, an aspect of Kate O'Brien's psychology as well. So many of this author's heroines have lost their mothers that the reader suspects she may be re-enacting her loss through them. Throughout her works the mother's death changes her child's life, and affects each of her characters differently but profoundly. Molly's death leaves Denis Considine with nothing to offset Anthony's pernicious hold; Reggie Mulqueen lives in terror of an empty life after Teresa dies; Angèle Maury recalls her Mother playing Phèdre as she imagines marrying her cousin. Clare seeks the love she had known in childhood, a love that comprised maternal nurturing and protection from the 'wet'. Luisa and Clare share this sense of familiar warmth; like Lucille and Fanny's, their attachment is more sisterly than romantic. We see them eat together, talk tenderly, drink wine, and behave affectionately. They touch, and occasionally they kiss (in women's writing, 'the kiss has vast metonymic responsibility'.)[9] But they are also mutually maternal. For example, when Luisa returns from her tour of South America, the two are reunited in Naples in a suite of rooms they love. The setting feels like home to them, filled with 'all their flowers and books and follies . . . with the wine and fruit and bread they brought for supper and for breakfast, with windows open to the sky and noise of Naples in May weather, it was indeed a habitable place' (251). The emphasis here is clearly on the hominess of the setting. Kate O'Brien enhances the mood:

> Clare poured the coffee, and came and sat on a rickety footstool by Luisa's knees.
> 'Have we two stopped talking at all since Tuesday night?'
> 'Sweet, we have. And we've slept a great deal.'
> 'Oh no! Not enough! Not enough sleep, Luisa. We'll have to catch up on that.'
> 'Ah! You look tired.' (251-2)

These rooms replicate for Clare her grandmother's cottage; Luisa's love replicates her grandmother's; and the coffee is the tea from her grandmother's bottomless pot. Thus, when Clare urges Luisa to sing 'a cradle song' (252), a mother's lullaby, she is asking Luisa to soothe her as her grandmother, the only mother she has known, would soothe her.

Clare's childhood, however, looms as a source of consternation as well as comfort. She compares herself to Miriam in Hawthorne's *The Marble Fawn*, dogged and tormented by guilt. Clare can never lose her other, earlier self with its moral teachings and conventions. Kate O'Brien reveals the young Clare Halvey most poignantly, and perhaps most appropriately, just after Clare has spent several days with Luisa:

> she was wearied by knowing herself to be too much alive, and as if she were a flame; nevertheless it was only one-half of her that lived to that degree and in relation to that image. Another Clare, the familiar one of always, was about

her usual business, and was able to watch this newcomer coolly enough from the wings. And the newcomer knew this, and knew it with a sense of relief that puzzled and sometimes saddened her. One does not change, she thought, one does not escape. The heart grows and learns indeed — and gladly, gladly . . . But so do other parts of soul and thought and reason — and they grow as had been expected, along the taught and fore-ordained direction; not away and outward from sequestered life . . . out of sight of herself. (253)

Rose, too, is torn between powerful internal feelings and external demands. Ravaged by the 'claimant loves' of René and Antonio, she learns, as Matt Costello did when he was torn between convention and desire, that 'the needs of the heart are at the mercy of conventions, fixed ideas, self protection, wilfulness, fear, and the thousand hard insistent claims and irrelevancies of general life' (306).

Clare speaks for herself and Rose when she defines her behaviour in terms that accord with their upbringing: 'If to be a bohemian is to have forsaken the moral standards of properly instructed people, then surely I am one?' (253). Thus, she has isolated herself from her past. Having gone to Ballykerin to watch her grandmother die, she discovers that she will never feel at home there again, no more than she feels at home in her new life. In Clare's painful self-recognition, we can hear perhaps the voice of Kate O'Brien about to exile herself from Ireland for a final time:

She was shocked at how difficult she found the primitive life of her own people, and it saddened her to realise that, *prima donna* or not, she could not ever live now the simple, clean, courageous and uncomforted life from which her grandmother was departing in holy and collected peace. (343)

Having left her past, Clare expects as little security from her female lover as Rose can expect from her man. She must heed her own advice: 'Be sane. It wasn't life; it was a few days only, a forbidden interlude. You know you're used to being alone, it's how you are best. You must possess your soul, and learn to pray again' (264). Alone, Clare can come to terms with the moral precepts that plague her. She, at least, is freed of the temptation to sin. Rose, however, may never be. As she embarks on a long operatic tour to be 'oceans away' from Antonio on the eve of his marriage, she deludes herself that her 'huge American offer is perhaps . . . God's way of showing mercy to my sins . . . removing me from — from an occasion of sin' (340). But she goes in the company of her avid American suitor, who has waited in the wings for her throughout much of the novel.

Yet Rose is troubled more by the hurt she has caused another human being than by her conduct. Her distress is as much about the change her desertion has inflicted on her young lover René as about her own self-inflicted loss of Antonio: 'If she had created such a hardness in René, against her intent, then she was to blame for what he was and might become' (340). Despite appearances, both she and Clare remain intensely moral; each subscribes to a moral credo of her own devising. Neither, however, can fully overcome the social codes of Ballykerin and Lackanashee. Although Clare may have no place there, Ireland has left its unmistakable mark. As the novel ends, only her painful separation from Luisa relieves her of her guilt:

> Was it not good to sit *alone* under city trees, and know that love, plaguy love, was far away, and could not touch you? Rose with her sick heart, would not agree. She was fleeing a temptation to which she would not yield, but she was running from its precious brilliance into a kind of polite twilight that could be at least as dangerous as a source of sin? [sic].
> Sin. The word came now from far enough away. Yet it was the word of all. (345-6)

Clare expresses not only Kate O'Brien's loneliness but also her hope. For though alone and, for the moment, loveless, Clare has her talent to develop, her art to improve. As she leaves for Dresden and Vienna, the promise of working under Thomas's baton and tutelage consoles her. Carrying 'her heavy book of songs', Clare moves on. Her art is a burden, but it, not love, will succour her.

Having revealed herself as an artist in the 'disguise of myth' of *As Music and Splendour,* Kate O'Brien leaves myth behind her. In the two non-fictional works published before her death in 1974 — *My Ireland* in 1962 and *Presentation Parlour* in 1963 — she speaks in her own voice about her country, her family, and her art. But she still holds onto the lesson of *As Music and Splendour* that, for the artist, only art abides. John Jordan tells us that before she died, Kate O'Brien had not only been working on her *Memoirs* but on *Constancy,*[10] a novel ironic in its title. Lorna Reynolds sees in the failed, unfulfilled talent of Signora Vittoria, 'the wine glass perpetually in the hand, the bottle forever at the elbow' (148), Kate O'Brien's last self-portrait, a 'caricature' of herself as the artist who had 'neglected' her art,[11] as the writer who could no longer muster her squandered gift. But surely Clare Halvey, with her 'heavy book of songs', her dedication to her music, is as faithful a portrait of Kate O'Brien's persistent artistic dream as Signora Vittoria is of its failure. Clare Halvey's songs attest that, to the end, Kate O'Brien believed that if love inevitably fails, art sustains.

Notes and References

PREFACE
(pp. xi-xviii)

1. Peter Costello, *The Heart Grown Brutal: The Irish Revolution in Literature, from Parnell to the Death of Yeats, 1891-1939* (Dublin: Gill and Macmillan, 1977), 241.

2. Eavan Boland, 'Daughter of the Middle-Classes', *Irish Times* 27 February 1987, 12.

3. Kate O'Brien, *My Ireland* (London: B. T. Batsford, 1962), 148. The quotation with which Kate O'Brien begins this passage comes from Santayana's *Persons and Places,* eds. William Holzberger and Herman Saatcamp, Jr. (Cambridge: MIT, 1986), 97-8.

4. Kate O'Brien, *Distinguished Villa* (London: Ernest Benn Ltd., 1926), 85.

5. Lorna Reynolds, *Kate O'Brien: A Literary Portrait,* Irish Literary Studies 25 (Gerrards Cross: Colin Smythe; Totowa: Barnes and Noble, 1987), 15-41.

6. Kate O'Brien, *Presentation Parlour* (London: Heinemann, 1963), 3.

7. Vivian Mercier, 'Kate O'Brien', *Irish Writing* 1 (1946), 98.

8. Review of *The Land of Spices,* in *The Spectator,* 14 Feb. 1941, 184.

9. Kate O'Brien, *English Diaries and Journals* (London: Collins, 1943), 47.

Chapter 1.
BIOGRAPHICAL SKETCH
(pp. 1-4)

1. Kate O'Brien, *Farewell, Spain* (London: Virago, 1985), x-xi.

2. Reynolds, *Portrait,* 39.

3. John Jordan, 'Kate O'Brien: First Lady of Irish Letters', *Hibernia* 14 May 1973, 11.

4. Reynolds, *Portrait,* 89.

5. Reynolds, *Portrait,* 132.

6. Jordan, 'First Lady', 11.

Chapter 2
WITHOUT MY CLOAK
(pp. 5-20)

1. Kate O'Brien, *Without My Cloak* (London: Virago Press, 1986). All page references will be cited parenthetically in the text.

2. Joseph Lee, *The Modernisation of Irish Society 1848-1918* (Dublin: Gill and Macmillan, 1973), 16.

3. John Galsworthy, *The Forsyte Saga* (New York: Charles Scribner's Sons, 1948). All page references will be cited parenthetically in the text.

4. Review of *Without My Cloak, Irish Times* 26 Dec. 1931, 2.

5. Vivian Mercier, 'Kate O'Brien', *Irish Writing* 1 (1946), 90.

6. Lee, 17.

Chapter 3.
THE ANTE-ROOM
(pp. 21-32)

1. Kate O'Brien, *The Ante-Room* (Dublin: Arlen House, 1980). All page references will be cited parenthetically in the text.

2. Sir George Rostrevor Hamilton, ed., *Essays by Divers Hands,* Transactions of the Royal Society of Literature 27 (London: Oxford, 1955), 35.

3. Mercier, 98.

4. Mercier, 89-94.

5. George Eliot, *The Mill on the Floss, The Best Known Novels* (New York: Modern Library, 1940), 725.

6. *Presentation Parlour,* 32.

7. Reynolds, *Portrait,* 118.

8. Reynolds, *Portrait,* 33.

9. Joan Ryan, 'Class and Creed in Kate O'Brien', *The Irish Writer and the City,* ed. Maurice Harmon, Irish Literary Studies 18 (Gerrards Cross: Colin Smythe; Totowa: Barnes and Noble, 1984), 130.

Chapter 4.
MARY LAVELLE
(pp. 33-46)

1. Kate O'Brien, *Mary Lavelle* (London: Virago, 1984). All page references will be cited parenthetically in the text.

2. Katie Donovan, *Irish Women Writers – Marginalised by Whom?* Letters from the New Island Series (Dublin: The Raven Arts Press, 1988), 20.

3. *Farewell, Spain,* 3.

Chapter 5.
PRAY FOR THE WANDERER
(pp. 47-58)
1. Kate O'Brien, *Pray for the Wanderer* (New York: Doubleday, 1938). All page references will be cited parenthetically in the text.
2. Evelyn Waugh, 'The Irish Bourgeoisie', review of *Pray for the Wanderer* in *The Spectator* 29 Apr. 1938, 768.
3. Mercier, 94.
4. Mercier, 94.
5. F.S.L. Lyons, *Ireland Since the Famine* (Glasgow: Fontana, 1975), 546.
6. Lyons, 546.
7. Lyons, 545.
8. Lyons, 546.
9. Joan Ryan, 'Women in the Novels of Kate O'Brien: The Mellick Novels', *Studies in Anglo-Irish Literature,* ed. Heinz Kosok (Bonn: Bouvier Verlag, 1982), 325.
10. Lyons, 546.
11. Terence Brown, *Ireland, A Social and Cultural History 1922-79* (Glasgow: Fontana, 1981), 152-4.

Chapter 6.
THE LAND OF SPICES
(pp. 59-72)
1. Brendan Flynn, 'A Meeting with Kate', *The Stony Thursday Book* 7 ([Limerick]: n.p., n.d.), 43.
2. Kate O'Brien, *The Land of Spices* (Dublin: Arlen House, 1982). All page references will be cited parenthetically in the text.
3. Michael O'Toole, 'Kate O'Brien's Limerick', *The Stony Thursday Book* 7, 25.
4. Kate O'Brien, 'Memories of a Catholic Education', *The Stony Thursday Book* 7, 28.
5. 'Memories', 28-32.
6. *Presentation Parlour,* 65 ff.
7. 'Memories', 28.
8. 'Memories', 28.
9. Brown, 170.
10. Lyons, 361.
11. Brown, 175.
12. *Pray for the Wanderer,* 3-4.
13. James Joyce, *A Portrait of the Artist as a Young Man* (New York: Viking, 1969), 172.

Chapter 7.
THE LAST OF SUMMER
(pp. 73-85)

1. Kate O'Brien, *The Last of Summer* (Dublin: Arlen House, 1981). All page references will be cited parenthetically in the text.

Chapter 8.
THAT LADY
(pp. 86-98)

1. Kate O'Brien, *That Lady* (London: Virago, 1985). All page references will be cited parenthetically in the text.

2. Gregorio Marañón, *Antonio Pérez* (New York: Roy, [1955?]) 84.

3. Lorna Reynolds, 'Kate O'Brien and the Pursuit of Love and Freedom', *The Stony Thursday Book* 7 ([Limerick]: n.p., n.d.), 22, and *Portrait,* 73.

4. Martin A.S. Hume, *Philip II of Spain* (London: Macmillan, 1927), 228.

5. J.H. Elliott, *Imperial Spain 1496-1716* (New York: Mentor, 1963), 257.

6. Marañón, 86, 85, 88, 212, 98, 93.

7. Marañón, 210.

8. Peter Pierson, *Philip II of Spain* (London: Thames and Hudson, 1975), 124.

9. William Thomas Walsh, *Philip II* (London: Sheed and Ward, 1937), 582.

10. In addition to the works of Walsh, Hume, Elliot, and Pierson, I found the following studies particularly useful to an understanding of Philip II and the historical episode on which *That Lady* is based: Geoffrey Parker, *Philip II* (Boston: Little Brown, 1978); R. Trevor Davies, *The Golden Century of Spain 1501-1621* (London: Macmillan, 1937).

11. See Marañón, 84 citing Gaspar Muro, *Vida de la Princessa de Eboli* (Madrid, 1877), 84.

12. Reynolds, *Portrait,* 70.

13. Kate O'Brien, *Teresa of Avila* (New York: Sheed and Ward, 1951), 82.

14. E. Allison Peers, ed., *The Complete Works of Saint Teresa of Jesus,* 3 vols. (New York: Sheed and Ward, 1946) vol. 3, 85-6.

15. Marañón, 91.

16. Parker, 135.

17. Marañón, 218.

Chapter 9.
THE FLOWER OF MAY
(pp. 99-111)

1. Kate O'Brien, *The Flower of May* (New York: Harper and Brothers, 1953). All page references will be cited parenthetically in the text.

2. Kate O'Brien, *As Music and Splendour* (New York: Harper and Brothers, 1958).

3. John Jordan, 'Kate O'Brien — A Note on Her Themes', *The Bell* 19.2 (1954), 56.

4. Lillian Faderman, *Surpassing the Love of Men: Romantic Friendship and Love Between Women from the Renaissance to the Present* (New York: William Morrow, 1981), 251.

5. Sharon O'Brien, '"The Thing Not Named": Willa Cather as a Lesbian Writer"', *Signs* 9.4 (1984), 584.

6. Faderman, 117.

7. Faderman, 117-18.

8. Faderman, 125.

9. Esther Newton, 'The Mythic Mannish Lesbian: Radclyffe Hall and the New Woman', *Signs* 9.4 (1984), 561.

10. Susan J. Rosowski, 'The Novel of Awakening', *The Voyage In,* eds. Elizabeth Abel, Marianne Hirsch, Elizabeth Langland (Hanover: University Press of New England, 1983), 49.

11. Rosowski, 49.

12. Nancy Cott, 'Passionlessness: An Interpretation of Victorian Sexual Ideology, 1790-1850', *Signs* 4.2 (1978), 233.

13. Sharon O'Brien, 584.

Chapter 10.
AS MUSIC AND SPLENDOUR
(pp. 112-23)

1. Kate O'Brien, *As Music and Splendour* (New York: Harper, 1958). All page references will be cited parenthetically in the text.

2. Reynolds, *Portrait,* 90.

3. Catharine Stimpson, 'Zero Degree Deviancy: The Lesbian Novel in English', *Writing and Sexual Difference,* ed. Elizabeth Abel (Chicago: University of Chicago Press, 1982), 257.

4. Bonnie Zimmerman, 'Exiting from Patriarchy: The Lesbian Novel of Development', in Abel, Hirsch, and Landland, 245.

5. Zimmerman, 253.

6. Newton, 566.

7. Newton, 575.

8. Nancy Chodorow, *The Reproduction of Mothering* (Berkeley: University of California Press, 1978), 200.

9. Adrienne Rich, *Of Woman Born* (New York: W.W. Norton, 1985), 242.

10. Stimpson, 246.

11. Jordan, 'First Lady', 11.

12. Reynolds, *Portrait,* 93.

Select Bibliography

Primary Sources
  1. Fiction: Novels and Plays
  Distinguished Villa: A Play in Three Acts, London: Ernest Benn Ltd., 1926.
  Without My Cloak, London: Heinemann; Garden City: Doubleday, 1931. London: Virago, 1986. Introduction by Desmond Hogan.
  The Ante-Room, London: Heinemann; Garden City: Doubleday, 1934. Dublin: Arlen House, 1980. Preface by Eavan Boland.
  Mary Lavelle, London: Heinemann; Garden City: Doubleday, 1936. London: Heinemann Pocket Edition, 1947. London: Virago, 1984. Introduction by Tamsin Hargreaves.
  Pray for the Wanderer, London: Heinemann; Garden City: Doubleday, 1938. Harmondsworth: Penguin Books, 1951.
  The Land of Spices, London: Heinemann; Garden City: Doubleday, 1941. Dublin: Arlen House, 1981. Preface by Lorna Reynolds. London: Virago, 1988. Introduction by Mary Flanagan.
  The Last of Summer, London: Heinemann; Garden City: Doubleday, 1943. Dublin: Arlen House, 1982. Preface by Benedict Kiely.
  That Lady, London: Heinemann, 1946. London: Virago, 1985. Introduction by Desmond Hogan. Published as *For One Sweet Grape,* Garden City: Doubleday, 1946.
  That Lady: A Romantic Drama, New York: Harper, 1949.
  The Flower of May, London: Heinemann; New York: Harper, 1953.
  As Music and Splendour, London: Heinemann; New York: Harper, 1958.

  2. Fiction: Short Stories
  'A Fit of Laughing', *The Bell* 18.4 (1952): 217-20.
  'A Bus from Tivoli', *The Stony Thursday Book* 7 [Limerick]: n.p., n.d. 14-18.

  3. Nonfiction: Books and Monographs
  Farewell, Spain. London: Heinemann; Garden City: Doubleday, 1937. London: Virago, 1985. Introduction by Mary O'Neill.
  English Diaries and Journals, London: Collins, 1943. (Reprinted in *Romance of English Literature,* ed. W.J. Turner, New York: Hastings House,

1944, 185-225; *The Heritage of English Literature.* London: Thames and Hudson, 1983, 161-217).

Teresa of Avila. Personal Portraits Series. London: Parrish; New York: Sheed and Ward, 1951. (Reprinted in *The Critic* 34.2 (1975), 26-51.

My Ireland, London: Batsford; New York: Hastings House, 1962.

Presentation Parlour, London: Heinemann, 1963.

4. Nonfiction: Essays, Newspaper Columns
'Return in Winter', *Contemporary Essays,* ed. Sylvia Norman, London: Elkin Mathews and Marot, 1933, 19-31.

'Fiction', regular book-review column, *The Spectator,* London, 1938-1945.

'Aunt Johnny', *London Calling,* ed. Storm Jameson, New York, London: Harper Brothers, 1942, 284-92. (Reprinted in altered form in *Presentation Parlour,* London: Heinemann, 1963. 115-22).

'Introduction', *Romance of English Literature,* ed. W.J. Turner, New York: Hastings House, 1944. 15-18.

'Voice of the Children', *Irish Digest* 43.3 (1952), 9-11.

'George Eliot: A Moralizing Fabulist' *Essays by Divers Hands,* ed. Sir George Rostrevor Hamilton. Transactions of the Royal Society of Literature 27, London: Oxford University Press, 1955, 34-46.

'As to University Life', *University Review* 1.6 (1955), 3-11.

'Writers of Letters', *Essays and Studies* 9 (1956), 7-20.

'Irish Writers and Europe', *Hibernia* Mar. 1965. (Reprinted in *The Stony Thursday Book* 7 [Limerick]: n.p., n.d. 36-7.)

'Avantgardisme — in Europe and Ireland: Writers meet in Rome', *The Irish Times* 21 Oct. 1965, 9.

'Long Distance', *Irish Times* 7 Aug. 1967, 12; 1 Jan. 1969, 12; 7 Apr. 1969, 8; 6 Oct. 1970, 10; 21 Apr. 1971, 12.

'Memories of a Catholic Education: A Fragment from Kate O'Brien's Last Work', *The Tablet* 4 Dec. 1976. 1177-79. (Reprinted in *Sunday Press* 2 Jan. 1977; *The Stony Thursday Book* 7. [Limerick]: n.p., n.d. 28-32.)

'Imaginative Prose by the Irish, 1820-1970', *Myth and Reality in Irish Literature,* ed. Joseph Ronsley, Ontario: Wilfrid Laurier University Press, 1977, 305-16.

'Two letters from Kate O'Brien to Mary Hanley', *Stony Thursday Book* 5 [Limerick]: n.p., n.d. 6-8.

Secondary Sources
1. Personal Reminiscences
Flynn, Brendan, 'A Meeting with Kate', *The Stony Thursday Book* 7 [Limerick]: n.p., n.d. 43-5. Enthusiastic recollection of KO'B's last visit to Spain.

Jordan, John, 'Kate O'Brien: A Passionate Talent'. *Hibernia* 30 Aug. 1974, 19. Obituary that includes the writer's recollections of KO'B.

Mulkerns, Val. 'Kate O'Brien: A Memoir', *The Stony Thursday Book* 7 [Limerick]: n.p., n.d. 48-53. Novelist warmly recalls her youthful meetings with KO'B.

2. Biographical Essays

Boland, Eavan, 'That Lady: A Profile of Kate O'Brien 1897-1974', *The Critic* 34.2 (1975), 16-25. Sympathetic account of KO'B's life that purports to uncover her 'humanity'. Raises important questions but dismisses them with rejoinders by members of KO'B's family.

Closter, Susan Vander, 'Kate O'Brien', *British Novelists, 1930-1959,* ed. Bernard S. Oldsey, Detroit, Michigan: Gale Research Company, 1983, 389-96. Vol 15.2 of *Dictionary of Literary Biography.* Intelligent, succinct discussion of KO'B's novels.

DiBernard, Barbara, 'Kate O'Brien'. *Dictionary of Irish Writers,* ed. Robert Hogan, Connecticut: Greenwood Press, 1979, 487-8. Terse summary of KO'B's early life and literary career. Too brief to be useful.

Jordan, John, 'Kate O'Brien; First Lady of Irish Letters Talks to John Jordan', *Hibernia* 11 May 1973, 11. Profile of KO'B at 75 years, combining Jordan's admiring perceptions with KO'B's comments.

O'Toole, Michael, 'Kate O'Brien's Limerick', *The Stony Thursday Book* 7 [Limerick]: n.p., n.d. 23-27. Previously published in *Cara* 12.6 (1980), 51-6. Concise description of late nineteenth- and early twentieth-century setting of KO'B's novels.

Walsh, Caroline, 'In Search of Kate O'Brien', *Irish Times* 14 Aug. 1981, 8. Short biographical sketch that emphasises places in Ireland associated with KO'B.

3. Criticism: Articles and Books on Kate O'Brien

Boland, Eavan, 'Kate O'Brien', *The Stony Thursday Book* 7 [Limerick]: n.p., n.d. 46-8. Brief discussion of *Without My Cloak, The Ante-Room, Mary Lavelle* and *The Land of Spices* that pays some attention to feminist themes.

'Daughter of the Middle Classes', *Irish Times* 27 Feb. 1987, 12. Short newspaper essay that argues for Kate O'Brien's contemporary relevance.

Dalsimer, Adele M., 'A Not So Simple Saga: Kate O'Brien's *Without My Cloak'*, *Eire-Ireland* 21.3 (1986), 55-71. An elucidation of the social milieu of *Without My Cloak* by comparison with Sean O'Faolain's *A Nest of Simple Folk* and John Galsworthy's *The Forsyte Saga.*

Feehan, Fanny, 'Kate O'Brien and the Splendour of Music', *The Stony Thursday Book* 7 [Limerick]: n.p., n.d. 38-43. A short, interesting discussion of KO'B's musical and operatic knowledge apparent in *As Music and Splendour*.

Jordan, John, 'Kate O'Brien — A Note on Her Themes', *The Bell* 19.2 (1954), 53-9. Focusing on *The Flower of May,* discusses the theme of painful love in KO'B's novels (except *As Music and Splendour*). Marred by disconcerting misprint that refers to *The Ante-Room* as 'The Flute-Room'.

Kiely, Benedict, 'Kate O'Brien: Prayer and Departure', *The Stony Thursday Book* 7 [Limerick]: n.p., n.d. 5-13. A short, engaging discussion of the novels' themes with the exception of *The Flower of May* and *As Music and Splendour*.

Mercier, Vivian, 'Kate O'Brien', *Irish Writing* 1 (1946), 86-100. Intelligent discussion of KO'B's life and selected works that argues for her position as a moralist and an Irish writer of 'Romance'.

Reynolds, Lorna, *Kate O'Brien: A Literary Portrait,* Irish Literary Studies 25. Gerrards Cross: Colin Smythe; Totowa: Barnes and Noble, 1987. The only previous full-length study of KO'B's works. Includes a brief consideration of her early life and family history. Discussions of individual novels are occasionally limited by a delicacy of approach. Fails to provide the bibliography listed in the table of contents.

'Kate O'Brien and the Pursuit of Love and Freedom', *The Stony Thursday Book* 7 [Limerick]: n.p., n.d. 19-23. Brief discussion of *The Ante-Room, The Land of Spices,* and *That Lady* that emphasises the characters' disappointing loves and their desire for freedom.

'The Image of Spain in the Novels of Kate O'Brien', *National Images and Stereotypes,* eds. Wolfgang Zack and Heinz Kosok, Tübingen: Gunter Narr, 1988, 181-8. Vol. 3 of *Literary Interrelations: Ireland, England and the World,* 3 Vols. Consideration of KO'B's use of Spain as an analogue to Ireland. Argues that Spain permits the development of the individual that Ireland inhibits.

Ryan, Joan, 'Class and Creed in Kate O'Brien', *The Irish Writer and the City,* ed. Maurice Harmon, Irish Literary Studies 18. Gerrards Cross: Colin Smythe; Totowa: Barnes and Noble, 1984, 125-35. Discussion of *Without My Cloak, The Ante-Room, The Land of Spices,* and *Pray for the Wanderer,* emphasising the importance of KO'B's depiction of the Catholic upper middle-class.

'Women in the Novels of Kate O'Brien: The Mellick Novels', *Studies in Anglo-Irish Literature,* ed. Heinz Kosok, Bonn: Bouvier Verlag, 1982, 322-32. Unfocused evaluation of KO'B's women characters and the limited choices provided by their Limerick milieu. Considers *Pray for the Wanderer* and *The Land of Spices*.

4. Criticism: References in General Studies

Cahalan, James, *The Irish Novel: A Critical History*, Boston: G.K. Hall, 1988, 208-12. Notes KO'B's analysis of The Irish Catholic middle-class and of relationships between women.

Costello, Peter, *The Heart Grown Brutal: The Irish Revolution in Literature, from Parnell to the Death of Yeats, 1891-1939*, Dublin: Gill and Macmillan; Totowa: Rowman and Littlefield, 1977, 268. A one-line reference to the banning of *The Land of Spices*.

Curtin, Chris, Riana O'Dwyer, and Gearoid O'Tuathaigh, 'Emigration and Exile', *Irish Studies: A General Introduction*, ed. Thomas Bartlett *et al.*, Dublin: Gill and Macmillan; Totowa: Barnes and Noble, 1988, 83. Refers to *Mary Lavelle* as part of a discussion of Irish writers and emigration.

Dawe, Gerald, D.E.S. Maxwell, and Riana O'Dwyer, 'Twentieth-Century Irish Literature', *Irish Studies: A General Introduction*, ed. Thomas Barlett *et al.*, Dublin: Gill and Macmillan; Totowa: Barnes and Noble, 1988, 189. A brief survey of KO'B's definition of the roles of Irish women.

Donovan, Katie, *Irish Women Writers – Marginalized by Whom?* Letters from the New Island Series, Dublin: Raven Arts Press, 1988, 19-23. Specious argument against feminist presses that insists that women writers must be considered only in relation to the male 'canon'. Juxtaposes individual female and male writers and compares *Mary Lavelle* with *A Portrait of the Artist as a Young Man*.

Fallis, Richard, *The Irish Renaissance*, Syracuse: Syracuse University Press, 1977, 228. Passing reference to KO'B as an impressive writer of realistic fiction.

Jeffares, A. Norman, *Anglo-Irish Literature*, Macmillan History of Literature, Dublin: Gill and Macmillan, 1982, 234-5. A brief survey of Kate O'Brien's novels and narrative style.

Kiely, Benedict, *Modern Irish Fiction – A Critique*, Dublin: Golden Eagle Books, 1950, passim. An important consideration of Irish fiction that considers KO'B in relation to its major themes: 'big houses', the provincial middle-class, history, exile, love, and religion.

Lawrence, Margaret, 'Matriarchs', *The School of Femininity*, New York: Stokes, 1936, 243-7. Considers KO'B as an Irish 'matriarch', emphasising the author's concern with family and Catholicism in *Without My Cloak* and *The Ante-Room*.

McHugh, Roger and Maurice Harmon, *Short History of Anglo-Irish Literature: From its Origins to the Present Day*, Dublin: Wolfhound Press, 1982, 259-62. Brief consideration of KO'B's novels with the exception of *The Flower of May* and *As Music and Splendour*. Emphasises KO'B's psychological acuity.

Scott, Bonnie Kime, 'Feminist Theory and Women in Irish Writing',

The Uses of the Past: Essays on Irish Culture, eds. Audrey S. Eyler and Robert F. Garratt, Newark: University of Delaware Press; London and Toronto: Associated University Presses, 1988. Argues for a 'gynocritical' reading of KO'B and other Irish women writers.

Index